Jobs Are Not the Answer—

But Then, What Is?

Published by
American Book Business Press™
An imprint of American Book Publishing
American Book Publishing
P.O. Box 65624
Salt Lake City, UT 84165
www.american-book.com

Printed in the United States of America on acid-free paper.

Jobs Are Not The Answer - But Then What Is?

Designed by Karen Maryanski, design@american-book.com

Publisher's Note: *This publication is designed to provide accurate and authoritative information in regard to the subject matter covered. It is sold or distributed with the understanding that the publisher and author is not engaged in rendering legal, accounting, or other professional service. If legal advice or other expert assistance is required, the services of a competent professional person in a consultation capacity should be sought.*

Library of Congress Cataloging-in-Publication Data is available upon request.

ISBN 1-58982-156-4

MacIntyre, Angus, Jobs Are Not The Answer—But Then What Is?

Special Sales

Jobs Are Not the Answer—
But Then, What Is?

Angus MacIntyre

The KLOG Centre
(The Kanata Learning Opportunities Growth Centre—www.klog.ca)

Dedication

I wish to dedicate this book to those who had a major part in influencing the person I am today. I had the pleasure of working closely with my father in the stove and furnace repair business for several years before he died when I was fourteen. Often when my buddies were at the movies on Saturday afternoon, I was learning to drive our truck or working inside an old coal furnace "bricking it up" because I was, in his words, "small enough to fit just about anywhere." Being a very religious man did not stop him from lecturing a priest on ethics when he felt the occasion called for it. He was a real innovator, having made all of the equipment in his workshop—including one of the first electric welders in the city. Maybe that's the reason I have a patent on an original "wood splitter."

Being number seven in a family of ten boys (although three died in infancy) meant my mother was never bored or worried about what to do in her spare time. We teased her constantly about her ability to disguise codfish. Her comment, "codfish gives you brains." Our answer was, "If that is the case, we must all be geniuses." As my friends, and those of my brothers, often remarked, "Your mother didn't raise seven boys, she raised three times that number, we had as much respect for her as we did our own mothers." When I was consoling a cousin on the loss of her mother, whom she was very close to, she responded, "Angus, I loved my mom dearly but I actually felt worse when your mother died." Both of my parents were active in the church, local food cooperative, credit union, People's School (part of the Antigonish Movement) and anything else to help the underdog or community. They were held in high respect by all who knew them.

There are a few others who stand out in my upbringing, it will come as a great surprise to them to realize the important part they played in my growth and development. I am talking about my brothers Alex, Chalmers, Charlie, Gilbert (a union organizer, now deceased), Carl—who taught me about the joy and dignity of work—and especially Lorne who has taught me so much about values and ethics, being of service to others, being clear on who you are and living life according to that knowledge.

Another early influence were the "Morrisons," Tippy (now deceased) and Joe, who owned the IGA grocery store where I worked my first job as a deliveryman, and their brother Maynard who worked for them. Tippy and Joe taught me about providing quality service to customers at a reasonable price, while appreciating the importance of a sense of humor, not only to laugh at others, but more importantly to laugh at ourselves. Maynard taught me the concept of "the customer is always right;" as he used to say, "Even when they're wrong, they're right." He also taught me lessons regarding the value of quality work, not to stop looking for work once I found a job, giving 100 percent and then some to the task at hand, and no matter how menial the task seemed to be, there was dignity in toiling for a living. They didn't know it at the time, but the other staff (back then we called them clerks) had a big influence as well. Mabel Munro, who knew the customers so well she could fill out 80 to 90 percent of the grocery orders for dozens of customers before they phoned them in on Monday mornings. Then there was Myrna Marchand, who packed every order as if it were going to her home because that's what she would want someone to do for her. Going home with my sides sore from laughing, there were many days when I felt work wasn't supposed to be that much fun—they should have charged me for working there.

Early in my work life I was fortunate to work with Mary M. Gillis, who undertook a labor of love as she taught me, often "on the job," almost everything I know about community development and the unique contribution each and every individual has to offer their community.

The last great influence I need to recognize is the great American person-centered therapist and educator, Karl Rogers. After reading everything he wrote and studying at the University of Texas under a colleague of his, who worked with him for fifteen years, I finally had the pleasure of spending three weeks with Karl at a person-centered workshop in Oakland, California. He was as genuine in person as he was in his writings. I was not disappointed. It was difficult to keep the conversation focused on him because he was always more interested in talking about me and the issues I was working on at the community level with the First Nations people in northern Canada.

Foreword

Early on in this humane and good-natured book, Angus MacIntyre notes that although joblessness is a terrible scourge, only 4 percent of people who are employed actually enjoy their jobs.

This is a shocking statistic and it underlies Angus's thesis that community economic development must go beyond the mere provision of employment. In fact, Angus sees community economic development as a means of attacking a range of global problems that are only beginning to capture the attention of policy makers and governments.

We who live in the western democracies are the wealthiest people in history—but we're deeply discontented. Our societies are increasingly inequitable; the rich get richer and the middle class vanishes. The quality of our environment—water, air, earth—have never been worse and an exploding world population exacerbates the problem.

Our communities are under attack and public services are deteriorating as our nation's collective wealth increases. People have lost confidence in institutions which purport to offer leadership. Government, education, business, churches, the professions—their failures are in the headlines every day. We don't even have a sound sense of what social well-being is, nor how we might measure or create it.

Should we just slit our wrists and be done with it?

Not according to Angus MacIntyre. Relentlessly upbeat and cheerful, Angus has a wealth of experience with communities of every kind, having worked in both rural and urban communities across North America. He believes, as I do, that an ordinary person helps change the world by taking action to defeat injustice, poverty, and despair in his or her own small corner of the globe. Angus knows that changes are possible because he has helped communities achieve them, over and over again.

Think globally, act locally. That's what we used to say thirty-five years ago. To which I would add, share your reflections on what you've learned. That's what Angus MacIntyre has done in the book you hold in your hand and we're all the richer for it.

Silver Donald Cameron
Box 555, D'Escousse, NS B0E 1K0
Phone (902) 226-3165, fax (902) 226-1904

Home page: http://www.islemadame.com/sdc/

Weekly newspaper columns: http://groups.yahoo.com/group/sdcns/join

Public speaking: http://www.atlanticspeakersbureau.com

"Harboring resentment is like giving yourself a dose of poison and waiting for the other person to die."

—Anonymous

Preface

This book is intended to open dialogue on the following questions: can we act with deeper meaning in life and work, can there be dignity in work, is meaningful public participation in the decision making process possible, what is real development, can we measure progress toward achieving the good life, and related questions. The context for the book is development on Cape Breton Island, on the eastern shore of Canada. Cape Breton Island has been in a state of underdevelopment (as characterized by unemployment rates of 20 to 50 percent, depending on whose figures you believe) for the past eighty years. Suffice to say the real figures are much higher than the official unemployment figures. Job creation efforts on Cape Breton Island the past forty years have produced few long-lasting results except to increase the amount of dependency on someone else solving the economic problems. Understanding the issue of dependency is critical if we are to successfully prepare ourselves for the challenges facing us. I suspect this is equally true for other underdeveloped regions or communities in a state of stagnation or decline.

It may help reading this book if you know how it is organized. The first two chapters are quite different from the rest of the book. Chapter one describes a consciousness-raising personal encounter I had when returning to my roots on Cape Breton Island after being away for a number of years. The second chapter is a story regarding insights I gained after several years of listening to the so-called "grassroots" people of Cape Breton Island—the people who are almost never consulted by the government or experts and even less often listened to.

The next three chapters are based on the assumption that if we are to emerge successfully from our present dilemma, we must understand "where we are," "how we got here," and identify "where we want to go" and "how we intend to get there."

Chapter six is intended to make a case for having new methods for measuring progress as it relates to well-being and sustainable development on a societal level by answering the question, "can we measure real progress in the affirmative."

I then describe four different experiences I had at the community level over the past thirty-six years, providing the opportunity for individuals, groups and communities to empower themselves and take control of development.

I follow up the case studies by answering the question, "why jobs are not the answer," and examine why work is so burdensome to many. I suggest the need for a new model of work. I ask the reader to think *outside the box* when examining the idea of the future of work.

In closing I suggest we have the option to empower ourselves to create our own future rather than just responding to the trends of the marketplace. The book ends with a plea to put people first in our efforts to achieve the "good life."

Introduction

On Sunday, January 21, 2001, Lloyd Robertson announced on Canadian Television's (CTV's) late-night news that 3,500 people in Oshawa, Ontario would be laid off at the General Motors plant and a further 5,000 people might be laid off at other automobile plants in Ontario. The cuts would have drastic effects on thousands of individuals and companies that supplied materials and parts to the factories.

The following day, Monday, January 22, 2001, the Canadian Broadcasting Company (CBC) announced that, according to the *Wall Street Journal*, Chrysler would announce as many as 21,000 job cuts over the next three years. The *Journal* reported sources close to the company, claiming Zetsche, the new CEO, would be announcing that 6,000 of Chrysler's 30,000 white-collar jobs, 10,000 to 15,000 of its 95,000 manufacturing workers and about 6 of its 41 plants would disappear in North America. If all the cuts were made it would mean a 17 percent reduction in Chrysler's North American workforce.

Closer to home, in Cape Breton, the *Oran*—the weekly paper for Inverness County—quoted the President of the Strait Area Chamber of Commerce from a letter to the new minister responsible for the Atlantic Canada Opportunities Agency. The Honorable Robert Thibault said, "It is time for serious development in Cape Breton, which lost over 4,000 jobs last year alone."

Several times a week, every week for the past few years, we heard similar announcements of hundreds of thousands of jobs being lost. It shouldn't have taken a great leap of faith to realize this was a reality many people faced and would continue to face. There simply weren't guarantees of long-term employment anymore. Thus, even those who did have jobs, were unable to see employment as being able to provide a secure and fulfilled life.

On Thursday, January 25, 2001, Penny Mosher, from the Canadian Business Development Bank in Halifax was interviewed on CBC's morning program. She quoted a survey of North Americans that found only 4 percent of the population was excited about going to work on Monday.

It was somewhat shocking to learn that only 4 percent of the people surveyed enjoyed their jobs. Many were discovering that jobs were not only no longer secure, but also consumed such a large part of their time, energy, and thoughts, that there remained very little space in their lives for friends, family, recreation, or community. There was also limited time for developing talents or interests that were unrelated to the immediate day-to-day demands of jobs.

Suppose we traded our present jobs for a more fulfilled lifestyle. How would we survive? What would happen to the economy? What would happen to our communities? Is it possible to have meaningful work and still contribute to an economically viable community?

Contents

Chapter One

You What? You Quit Your Job?

I returned to Cape Breton Island after an extended stay in northern Manitoba and northern Ontario where I worked in the field of community-based economic development. I accepted an interesting and challenging position as director of education with the Waycobah First Nation, on Cape Breton Island. It gave me the opportunity to be closer to family and friends, and to renew my interest in Scottish culture. My first Christmas "back home" (in east Lake Ainslie—or, as we say locally, "east L.A." —near Waycobah), I hosted a family get-together to get reacquainted with extended family members. During the party it came as a shock to learn from a nephew, Gilbert MacIntyre Jr., that he had quit his job years earlier because of a casual conversation we'd had. Gilbert had worked as a linesman with what was at that time a provincial crown corporation, the Nova Scotia Power Commission. His job was as secure as any job in the province could be, it paid well and Gilbert liked the work. I wondered what had possessed him to quit and what I could have said to cause such a drastic reaction. Gilbert asked me if I remembered the encounter. I had a vague recollection of the exchange but certainly didn't think I influenced him to quit his job. So, I asked him to tell me what happened. Apparently, we had a chance meeting late one night and the conversation went something like this.

Angus: Hi, Gilbert, what's happening?

Gilbert: Oh, not much. Just heading back to Halifax in time for work in the morning.

Angus: Great. How's Karen (Gilbert's wife) and the kids?

Gilbert: Fine, they're fine. Not happy with me only getting home every second weekend, but other than that, just fine. What's up with you? Where are you heading this time?

Angus: I'm off to do some work with the Union of New Brunswick Indians. I have to be in Fredericton for a ten o'clock meeting.

Gilbert: Say, Angus, what is it you do, anyway? You change jobs every couple of years and are always doing something interesting.

Angus: Oh! I'm a freelance concept generator.

Gilbert: You're a what?

Angus: A freelance concept generator.

Gilbert: What in the name of "h-e-double-hockey-sticks" is a freelance concept generator? I don't have a clue what you're talking about. What does it mean?

Angus: It really doesn't mean anything. That's a title a friend and fellow consultant coined as a lark in order to impress bureaucrats and academics—in other words, to "snow" them without saying anything.

Gilbert: So what do you do?

Angus: Well, in true Cape Breton tradition, the best way to explain it is to tell you a story. When Dawn Michelle (my oldest daughter) was in grade seven, she came home from school one day and said the teacher had asked her class what their parents did for a living. "Oh," I said, "that's an interesting question; what did you tell her?" "Well," she said, "I thought for a while and said my mom is a full-time mom and my dad goes to an awful lot of meetings and helps people." "Is that right," said the teacher. "Well, that's interesting. Your mom no doubt has her hands full but what exactly does your dad help people with?" So, I asked Dawn Michelle, "And what did you say? I'm curious about your answer." "Well," she said, "I thought real hard for a minute and said, 'He helps them with whatever is bothering them.' Well, Dad, how did I do?" "Dawn Michelle," I said, "you couldn't have explained it any better."

Gilbert: But what do you do about security? How do you know you're going to have a regular paycheck? How can you afford to change jobs every couple of years?

Angus: What job security does anyone have? The only security for me is to know who I am and be clear on my values and what is important to me. What's the most important thing to you?

Gilbert: Why, my family, of course.

Angus: Then why aren't you spending more time with them?

Gilbert: I have to make a living—I have to provide for them. I owe it to them to provide a steady income. What kind of a stupid question is that, anyway? Isn't it obvious why I have to work?

Angus: You say your family is most important to you and it is especially important for you to spend time with your kids while they are young. Under the present circumstances, you are missing a good part of their childhood and that doesn't please you, correct?

Gilbert: Yeah, but what choice do I have?

Angus: I can't give you the answer to that question. I would ask you to think about whether or not your behavior—what it is you are actually doing—is congruent with what you say you believe. You say your family is the most important thing to you but you act as if your

	job is the most important thing to you. Yes? No?
Gilbert:	You're being very difficult and not at all helpful. What do I do about security and providing an income for the family? Besides, I like my job and I'm damn good at it.
Angus:	I don't doubt that for a moment. But, first of all, no job is ever totally secure. Secondly you could lose your job tomorrow due to circumstances beyond your control. How will you explain to your kids when they are grown that you missed their childhood because you loved them so much you couldn't be with them?
Gilbert:	Yeah! Exactly. That's my dilemma.
Angus:	Well, good luck. As you can see, I am far better at formulating questions than I am at providing answers. Besides, I don't really think you want me to tell you what to do.
Gilbert:	Yes I do; then I can blame you when it doesn't work out. Well, thanks a lot. Thanks for nothing. The next time I have a problem I don't want an answer to, I'll be sure to get in touch with you.

Gilbert continued the story. "Well, that is pretty much how it happened. On my way back to Halifax I gave a lot of thought to our conversation and it was at that point I decided I would no longer continue in my present employment but would move home to be closer to the family. I didn't have a clue what I was going to do. After some temporary part-time work as a linesman, I eventually got an interview for a firefighter position with the city of Sydney, Nova Scotia. The job paid about half what I used to make but I gladly accepted the position. One nice benefit is I get to follow in Dad's footsteps, becoming active in our labor union.

"The rest is history and it's been terrific. I took special training, on a voluntary basis and became an education officer with the Sydney Fire Department. I give talks to school children and community organizations regarding fire safety issues. A six-year-old I taught fire safety to was recognized nationally and internationally for saving himself, his brother and his mother from a fire at his home. Since then, I became the only Canadian asked by the National Fire Protection Association (NFPA) in Boston, MA to help launch their new safety curriculum for schools. I was a guest speaker for the Mississippi Association of Public Safety Educators at their state conference. I have also studied critical incident stress disorder and belong to a provincial team to help firefighters deal with high stress calls. We've been called in on everything from motor vehicle accidents, to fire calls, to calls relating to the Swiss Air disaster. It sure makes you feel good when you know you have made a difference in people's lives.

"But more important than anything else, I know my kids. I'm not the same guy who traveled the roads stringing line. I'm not as hard or as insecure. I know who I am and what I like. My two girls got something their brother didn't, to see their father walk into their school in a uniform, as someone who is respected; that's a nice memory to have. I'm healthier physically, mentally and spiritually. Life just doesn't get any better and what I really understand is, as long as I realize my self-worth isn't in what I have or what I do to make a living, life is always good. I couldn't be happier. Quitting my job was the best thing I ever did."

A short time after Gilbert left his former job, the Nova Scotia Power Commission was privatized and they laid off several hundred workers. Gilbert could have been one of them.

Chapter 2

If Only I Had a Job, All My Problems Would Be Solved

How It All Began

As mentioned earlier, in March 1995 I returned to Cape Breton Island after spending ten years in northern Manitoba and northern Ontario. I worked in the field of community-based economic development at the municipal level. As I reintegrated myself into community life in Cape Breton, I became aware of what appeared to be a prevailing attitude among Cape Bretoners: that, somehow, if someone would only give them a job, their problems, and by extension the problems of Cape Breton, would be solved. My hunch was people's attitudes about economic development and job creation were influenced by their perception of how the issues impacted them personally. I also suspected some people perceived themselves as having little influence or control over local economic conditions and this belief influenced their attitudes toward local development and employment issues.

The idea "jobs" were the answer to regional woes seemed to also prevail among political and community leaders, as well as the professionals assigned to work on economic development issues. My experience over the years suggested that a job, just any job, was not the answer to the problem of economic underdevelopment on Cape Breton Island.

I decided to use every opportunity to query the attitudes and opinions held by local people regarding the topics of economic development and employment, in an effort to obtain a clearer picture. It is my nature to encourage dialogue concerning community issues and my questions invariably stimulated discussion and further inquiries. The discussions were widespread, involving friends, acquaintances and strangers, as well as officials and leaders I encountered in my daily activities. For the most part, I talked with common folk, those often referred to as "grassroots." I quickly learned my questions were of great interest to people, or, more importantly, to those I listened to.

Since 1995, I have recorded the results of conversations with approximately one hundred and fifty people in more than a dozen Cape Breton Island communities. Most of the communities were rural villages, their populations varied in terms of ethnic descent. They included Whycocomagh, Waycobah, Waymatcook, Scotsville, Margaree Harbour, Margaree Forks, Cheticamp, Pleasant Bay, Bay St. Lawrence, Ingonish, Baddeck, Inverness, Mabou, Port Hood, St. Peters, and Big Pond—all centers where I was either working or visiting friends, relatives and colleagues. To a lesser degree, I recorded discussions with people from the towns of Port Hawkesbury, Sydney Mines, Glace Bay, and Louisbourg—communities that were experiencing serious economic difficulties. The intent of my questions was not to provide or even to find answers to the economic or social ills of Cape Bretoners. My purpose was to gain insight into what people thought of local economic conditions and what, if anything, they were prepared to do about the conditions.

How I Identified the Concerns

I undertook my research when given the opportunity to speak informally with "grassroots" people. The interviews were conducted when I visited a village or town for social or cultural gatherings (weddings, social visits, funerals, cultural events and so on) or for recreation (such as playing golf or volleyball). The context in which I worked was always a "natural" one; that is, I did not try to transform a real-life situation into an artificial research setting. Neither did I take on the formal identity of researcher or outside expert. I wanted to interact as one of them.

After listening to people talk about "jobs" or the "lack of jobs" over a period of six months, I found certain themes recurring regularly. It was at this point I decided to develop a series of questions designed to encourage people to talk more freely about their attitudes and feelings concerning economic development and unemployment. My approach was influenced by the work of one of my university professors, Michael Patton, on qualitative methodology. Patton authored three important publications dealing with the use of qualitative surveys and questionnaires as a method of behavioral science research. His basic premise is that qualitative techniques—such as interviewing people without setting up a formal interview time and place or using a formalized survey or questionnaire—are valid methods of inquiry. He also believes the results have as much credibility as, and in some cases more than, traditional methods of social-science research.

An informal interview is, by definition, interactive. This means the exchange cannot be rigidly structured, nor can all questions be preordained, since the responses themselves influence the course of discussion. I used each of my questions as a guideline when talking with people throughout Cape Breton. This approach allowed them to control and direct the flow of the conversation. I asked probing questions (like those in the dialogue that follows) in response to their statements, opinions or expressions of interest in a specific area; this invariably led to a deeper exploration of the issues under discussion. I was careful, however, to ensure certain pivotal concerns were raised systematically with all respondents.

Nothing was recorded at the time of discussion but I frequently made notes afterward. In fact, at the time of my conversations, I had no expectation of writing for publication. It was only "after the fact" I realized it might be useful and important to share some of the insights with others interested in the same issues.

What I Discovered about Local Views and Attitudes

I asked a variety of questions. One set of questions focused on employment preferences and a second set centered on economic development. I also asked people for their general aspirations for family and community as they related to economic concerns. After approximately a year and a half of conducting informal interviews, patterns became evident and I began to gain insight into how people felt about these important issues. The queries and responses are discussed in some detail below.

Employment Preferences

As the research proceeded, a general pattern of response emerged. The following composite portrait reflects typical dialogue on the subject of employment preferences.

Question: Hi, there. What's happening?
Response: Oh, nothing, nothing at all.

Question: Why not?

Response: There's no work. I haven't worked in months/years.

Question: There's not much going on here, eh?

Response: No, not since I got laid off…

Question: I assume if you had a job, it would solve all of your problems?

Response: Yeah, it sure would. If I only had a job, all of my problems would be over.

Question: Let's assume for a minute you have a job. What else would you need to be content or happy?

Response: Nothing, really. I would be satisfied with a job.

Question: Would it matter what kind of a job?

Response: No, not really, as long as it's work.

Question: So, a job paying minimum wages would be okay with you?

Response: Well, heck, no. It would have to pay enough to provide a decent living for me to support my family and to provide for my kids' future education.

Question: Oh! So, if you had a job that paid a reasonable wage, what else would you want the job to do for you, if you had a choice?

Response: Nothing. A good-paying job would satisfy me.

Question: So, given a choice, it wouldn't matter to you if you were slinging hamburgers at McDon-

	ald's or working in a factory doing routine work?
Response:	Oh yeah, well, given a choice, I would like to do something useful, something I am interested in.
Question:	So if you had a job that paid well and it was interesting work, you would be perfectly happy?
Response:	Absolutely.
Question:	You wouldn't need or want anything else?
Response:	No, absolutely not.
Question:	And if you had this perfect job, how long would you like to see it last?
Response:	Well, indefinitely, of course. There is nothing worse than these temporary, make-work projects. They teach bad work habits and never lead anywhere. Six months later you're back where you started.
Question:	So if you had a job—a well-paying, meaningful, permanent job—your problems would be solved and you would be happy?
Response:	Well, the obvious answer should be yes but I hesitate to say that, because I know you are going to come up with another question that is going to make me think about my answer, right?
Comment:	You've got that right. I've been found out.

These discussions often began when people complained about the lack of jobs or job opportunities on Cape Breton

Island. This suggested that most people merely wanted any kind of job. When earnestly invited to elaborate on their feelings, they revealed they wanted more. They wanted long-term, meaningful work. During this process I learned to pay close attention to the way I asked a question. It was quite an insight to learn that the way a question was framed often determined the kind of answer received.

Defining Economic Development

I initiated the discussion by asking people what they thought economic development was. When discussing employment, they often began by complaining, in general, about someone "out there" not bringing "jobs" to their community.

These informal interviews illustrated that most people thought economic development was about recruiting new industry to a region. In almost every instance, they thought of these new industries as factories or manufacturing plants. They did not relate the type of industry to any of Cape Breton's natural resources, except in a few instances when some expressed hope for a small fish plant. As one person, who had done some thinking about job creation, expressed it, "From what I have been reading, I know we shouldn't be chasing smokestacks but it would be nice to get a factory, probably a warehouse with computers in it, without the smokestack. I guess that's what this new global economy is all about."

Most people did not talk about the need to help existing businesses and industries or the desirability of creating new local business. A considerable number felt any attempt by a local person to "make it" in the business world would be met with jealousy and suspicion, rather than support and encouragement. Several people expressed this attitude, using exactly the same words: "We are our own worst enemy."

Responsibility for Economic Development

I would often follow up by asking, "Who should be responsible for economic development?" More than half did not know who was currently responsible for economic development, nor did they have an opinion on who should be responsible. Many who did have an opinion said their local politician was responsible; while others said "government" was responsible. No one I spoke to considered the economic condition of their community or region their responsibility.

Most were unfamiliar with the agencies mandated to promote economic development in their community or region. Few knew any details regarding the programs or services available in the region to help people start businesses or create jobs. Only three individuals reported firsthand experience with any of the agencies directly responsible for economic development and their experiences were not positive.

In the first case, a couple wanted to experiment with a new agricultural product. They were shuttled from one agency to another—local, regional and provincial. In their estimation, they weren't given any help, information or encouragement. They were continually told their idea did not make sense and would never work. The couple has operated their business successfully for several years and is currently exporting their product internationally. As one of them said, "We have been successful at doing this in spite of the agencies that are supposed to help, not because of them."

The second case differs somewhat. The individual was successful in getting into a government program designed to help new businesses. The problem he encountered, however, was an apparent lack of understanding and support from the entrepreneurial development agencies that were supposed to assist him. The person noted he was often referred from one employee to another and from one agency to another; thus it took months to get an answer to a simple question. The business counseling he received consisted of government employees telling him what he did or did not need and under what conditions he would receive help. When the conditions did not meet the needs of his business, he was told: "Take it or leave it. You are getting it for nothing, anyway." He felt the agency staff viewed him as ungrateful when he questioned the conditions under which he could receive assistance. He finally refused the financial help, to which he was entitled, rather than change his business plan in order to meet the government's criteria. This man now runs a successful business in Cape Breton and is exporting his product to the United States, as well.

The third case involved a professional proofreader and music teacher. After offering these services part-time for several years she decided to expand the music and editing services and include a third service, complementary to the other two, and establish all three as a new business. In addition to being a qualified candidate for a federal Human Resource Development Commission (HRDC) program, she was also referred to a local (nongovernmental) development agency designed to help people set up their own business. The individual explained to agency personnel her current situation and why she wanted to expand her business with a new, value added, service. She spent four months establishing eligibility, meeting program criteria, attending an information session and receiving guidance in preparing a market-feasibility study, financial forecasts and numerous other areas pertaining to the correct completion of the required business plan. After a final scolding for taking so long to complete her business plan, the candidate was informed that because she already offered two of the services, which were considered no more than just hobbies in the eyes of this bureaucrat, she was not eligible for the program. She was so devastated by the treatment she received, she gave up on the idea, citing it was too time consuming and frustrating dealing with all the bureaucracy. She gradually recovered some of the drive to establish the business and decided to try again, this time without seeking help from government or development agencies. She is currently developing the business as originally planned.

Public Involvement in Economic Development

To gain further insight into the public's ideas of their personal responsibility in their communities, I asked further questions. For example, I asked people if they had ever been involved in discussions regarding future economic development in their community or region. A few had heard of local public meetings about economic development but had not taken an interest in attending the sessions. Most people, however, thought it was a good idea to have organized meetings on the subject. Many felt it was beyond their ability to understand what made an economy tick or how they could be involved in economic activity. They felt economic development and job creation should be left to the experts and they identified government staff, university teachers, business leaders and consultants as experts. The vast majority felt they had nothing of value to offer. Only a few stated that, if approached, they would volunteer to assist with problem solving related to the issue.

Funding Economic Development

When I asked, "Who should fund economic development?" those interviewed almost unanimously said the responsibility belonged to the federal government, followed closely by the provincial government. A number of people felt local government should not be directly responsible for economic development; they feared it would lead to a rise in local taxes. They thought municipal politicians should fight for grants from the provincial and federal government, rather than devoting scarce local resources to problems beyond local influence or control.

No one thought private industry could be expected to take responsibility for creating jobs. Industry was seen to be in the business of making a profit; therefore, employing fewer people would be its goal. Many cited banking institutions as the epitome of corporate profit-seeking. Local people could not identify a major corporation concerned with social issues or economic development in their area. Several small local firms, however, were seen as concerned with local conditions. The firms were often generous when asked to support a local cause, providing funds, material goods or volunteers. They were perceived as having a commitment to the well-being of the local community.

The Economic Future—Discouragement And Hope

When asked whether economic conditions would improve in the foreseeable future, the general belief expressed was that the situation would worsen in the immediate future. They could not envision a day when Cape Breton could achieve an unemployment rate less than 10 percent. No one believed the unemployment figures reported in the media. Many thought the real rate of unemployment to be two or three times the figures being used by the experts.

Nearly all said they would not discourage their friends or relatives from leaving the island, nor would they encourage migrants to return to Cape Breton, except to retire. Almost everyone had a story about at least one friend or relative who had recently left Cape Breton. Within a ten-mile stretch of road, one individual identified eight families that had moved in the previous months.

On the basis of these conversations, it became obvious to me that people felt angry, powerless and discouraged about Cape Breton's economic prospects for the near future. They saw local economic problems as deriving from "those government bean counters that make decisions about our communities and our lives, which they know nothing about."

Within these negative expressions, however, I was able to find a spark of hope. It came at a moment of insight, when I realized what lay beneath the complaints and criticisms. People's complaints were, after all, focused on conditions they felt very strongly about. Though they saw harm being done and felt solutions were beyond their control, they cared deeply about their situations and communities.

It would be incorrect to read the data thus far as an indication of indifference, apathy, dependency or ineptitude. On the contrary, when questions were framed in a manner that gave people a chance to imagine how circumstances could be better, they quickly began to describe what could be done. People identified highways, water and sewer, education and health care as areas where great savings could be realized, if the government consulted local communities before making decisions. One person described how he spent seven days in a hospital at a cost of $1,500 per day—not because he was ill, but because it was the only way his doctor could get him to Halifax (in an ambulance—which he also didn't need) without a two-month delay for a test he needed.

Tourism was often cited as an area where the existing strategy could be improved. The feeling was, if consultation with local people became the first concern in designing improvements in signage, roads, scenic lookouts, picnic facilities and developed waterfronts, tourism would increase. More tourists would come, not merely because of the improvements but to experience the local "way of life."

Family And Community

I asked, "Given a meaningful choice, what would you want for your family and community?" This "leading question" opened the way for interactive interviews, like those about employment preferences. While the context of the conversation was economic development, the response was often much broader than the economy or jobs. People talked about the importance of maintaining a local school, saying the school was the heart of a community. Their arguments with local school boards had as much to do with the quality of education and whether or not it prepared their children for the world they would live in, as it did with economies of scale—whether bigger was better, or whether more was better or even necessary!

They often talked about the importance of music and dance, not in economic terms, but in terms of the culture and the maintenance of local values. Although more and more economists highlight the important economic impact of cultural activities on communities, many individuals felt the activities had intrinsic value and it was not right to evaluate them in strictly economic terms.

For instance, the Celtic Colors International Festival, held in October 1997 throughout Cape Breton Island, resulted in positive comment, not because it was an economic success or extended the tourist season but it gave local communities an opportunity to come together and celebrate their spirit, which many felt was still alive and well.

People told me that part of the tradition of Cape Breton is its strong history of self-reliance and independence, something several felt was being eroded. The essence of the responses I received wherever I went was this: people want their communities to have sustainable development, leading to independence and self-reliance. The majority of people I talked to did not want progress at any price. They wanted to keep many of their traditional values. They recognized that to do so, they also had to sustain their community's economic well being. Still, most looked to the government to answer the question for them.

Chapter 3

The Past: How we got where we are today

Since the 1960s, Canada has become increasingly and dangerously divided geographically, politically, socially and culturally. The winds of change have been blowing, particularly in the past decade. Democratization of communist countries, the fall of the Iron Curtain, budget and trade deficits, the Persian Gulf, infrastructure decay, tax and the attitudes of all levels of government, a new world order, education and labor force deficiencies, government gridlock, global warming, the pace of technological change, the relationship with native people in Canada, the decline of rural areas, our urban crises, a united Germany, changing means of capital formation, waste management, economic restructuring, the saving and loans crises in the U.S., have created serious dilemmas. These are only a few of the major structural changes and developments that have faced us in recent years. Major changes like these will continue to unfold and how we adjust to changing situations will largely shape the direction of economic development at all levels—global, national, provincial and local.

At the same time, the changes and our adjustments to them will dictate how and to what extent economic progress can be achieved at the community level. After all, this is where the action is and what holds the greatest promise for restructuring. It seems clear: change and adjustment to changing conditions should be a dominant characteristic of this century. What will world, national, provincial or local conditions be like by the year 2020? Of course, predictions are difficult because massive changes and adjustments create widespread uncertainty, an uncertainty that will be a dominant characteristic of this new millennium.

While I am convinced Adam paused at one point in the Garden of Eden to say, "Eve, we are living in a period of transition," I am also convinced the world was changed forever since September 11, 2001 and the World Trade Center disaster. I believe no thinking person would assert that earlier centuries experienced change as the twentieth century has. While change has been a characteristic of all generations, the speed of change we are now experiencing is entirely different. In a world buffeted by change, faced daily with new threats to its safety, the only stability possible is stability in motion. Being able to constantly adapt to or control change is about renewal and renewal is not just about change. It is also the process of bringing the results of change into line with our values and purposes.

The changes in structural conditions combined with an environment of uncertainty will lead to unpredictable results. These challenges can be perceived as obstacles or as opportunities. The Chinese have an interesting word for crisis: half the word means danger—the other half, opportunity. It is as though a mountain of obstacles and opportunities have suddenly been placed in the path of our progress. The challenge is for us to create a developmental process to provide us with the means to get over, around or through the mountain. Which half we choose to emphasize will determine our future.

A story told by a neighbor on Lake Ainslie clearly demonstrates this point. My neighbor was standing by his fence when a stranger approached him.

Stranger:	Hi, there, how are you today?
Neighbor:	Just great—how about yourself?
Stranger:	I'm fine, thanks. I am thinking about moving to this community and would like to know what the people are like here?
Neighbor:	Well, what are the people like where you live now?
Stranger:	Oh, there're not the greatest. They are difficult to get along with—always bitching and complaining about their neighbors, nobody works together, they don't get involved in the community and leadership is poor.

Neighbor: You will find people here with many of the same negative characteristics—just about the same as they are back there.

Some time later, another stranger came along, saying he was thinking of moving to the community. He asked my neighbor the same question regarding what the local people were like.

Neighbor: What are the people like where you come from?

Stranger: Generally speaking, they are very friendly, helpful and good neighbors. People tend to look out for one another and have a real sense of community. It is a good place to live.

Neighbor: You will find the local people and the community here similar to the one you are leaving.

A short anonymous poem makes the same point. "Two men looked out from prison bars, the one saw mud, the other stars."

History of Past Efforts

The history of regional development in Canada over the past forty years has been characterized by three approaches—or more properly, three nonindigenous theories and policies. The principal characteristics are as follows:

(1) Interregional Development (1960s)
- Removal of dependency on labor
- Capital mobility to its most productive use
- Unemployment and low wages should not be alleviated but take their natural course
- Encourage a perfectly competitive market
- Economic structures are given
- Individuals must adapt to the forces of the market

(2) Compensatory (1970s)
- Transfer payment (equalization, unemployment insurance, welfare) rather than real economic development
- Don't change underlying economic context
- Compensate for underdevelopment with large expenditures for unemployment insurance, equalization and regional development

(3) Development (1980s to 1990s)
- Change economic underpinnings of the region
- Plan urban-centered growth
- Encourage economic competition and specialization away from major centers in Canada and the province
- Support capital subsidies both directly (grants and tax concessions) and indirectly (physical infrastructure)

The outcomes of past efforts were questionable; they tended to attract what can best be described as footloose industries with no real commitment or loyalty to a local community. This was not only true for Cape Breton Island but for other parts of Canada and the United States as well. As I traveled extensively in my consulting work over the years in northern Canada and the eastern United States, time and time again local people repeated stories of companies who came to their community because of government grants or tax concessions and left just as quickly when the source of free capital dried up.

The results of the government's efforts were:

- A fraction of the jobs went to locals
- New outside business tended to crowd out existing firms by increasing wages
- Production often shifted from another region of Canada
- Economic decisions were made outside the region.

There has been little analysis or evaluation of the efforts expended to deliver regional development programs and services of the federal or provincial governments. Studies that have been done seem to get buried in bureaucracy and never see the light of day. As well, authors of these documents only tell the people who fund the "report" what they want to hear. In other words, they try not to be too critical of the agency carrying out the project, because it is the same group that is paying them for the assessment.

The Issue of Dependency

Another shortcoming of solving the problem of regional disparity is the issue of dependency. It has never been addressed by the government's approach to regional development. The idea that development must rely almost entirely on outside investment leaves the region ripe for exploitation. Although the specifics of regional development have changed under the new regional development initiatives, the policy of giving has not. We have raised the "ante" (grants, tax concessions) but we have not learned much from the past failure of looking to someone else to solve our problems. Much of the approach of relying on outside investment contravenes sound principles of local economic development, which require a balance of outside and local investment.

Despite major initiatives by both federal and provincial governments, which have put billions of dollars into this region of the province, the Cape Breton economy is still largely dependent on outside forces and assistance. After a history of boom and bust, Cape Bretoners recognize the need to lessen the impact of uncontrollable external forces on the local economy and its people. The highly unstable world resource markets have historically meant that the economy of Cape Breton Island has been buffered by unpredictable and often difficult changes. The large amount of capital required for resource development has meant business decisions affecting the regional economy have been shaped, at least in part, by forces external to conditions on Cape Breton Island. As well, federal and provincial agreement policies, often influenced by political forces external to this region, have eroded local control and responsibility.

In order to correct the situation, a new approach is required. The approach with the greatest chance of turning things around will be one that relies on local efforts. The development of a community-based economic strategy with the active participation and commitment of key people in each sector of the local economy has the greatest chance of success.

The development of short- (one to three years) and long- (five to ten years) range goals for each sector of the local economy is but a first step in this process. Research and development initiatives must be undertaken that will provide the technological know-how not just to survive but to direct the future as we enter the twenty-first century.

A developmental approach with different characteristics than past efforts seems in order. This approach would imply:

- Developing a better understanding of history and what is happening now
- Developing the skills necessary to build a community economy
- Encouraging the evolution of community democracy by awakening a community's resourcefulness

- Finding new ways to finance businesses based on new ethics and values
- Working with nature and not against her
- Preparing a proactive approach to directing future economic activities.

If we are really interested in working toward a vital society with the capacity for constant renewal, we must depend upon the energy, purpose and creativity of its individual members; only individuals can produce a society open to innovation and renewal. In his thoughtful and wide-ranging book, *Self-Renewal: The Individual and the Innovative Society*, John W. Gardner, who was secretary of state for health, education and welfare under President Kennedy, discusses the characteristics of the self-renewing individual: flexibility, independence, and perhaps most importantly, motivation—a capacity for self-development and self-knowledge. He also explores the forces and habits of mind which hamper personal growth, ranging from fear of failure to the comfortable web of the accustomed.

Dr. Gardner expresses that today's mass society provides a wide expanse of choice and opportunity and the largest possible framework for individual self-realization, even though it sometimes threatens creativity and the capacity for self-renewal. He urges each individual to identify with values beyond self, to believe in something, care about something, stand for something. Dr. Gardner insists there is, and always has been, a basic consensus on values and attacks the fashionable attitude of moral neutralism.

Each generation must rediscover the meaning of its society's values. In his eloquent conclusion, Dr. Gardner states that, instead of giving young people the impression their task is to stand a dreary watch over the ancient values, we should be telling them the grim but bracing truth: it is their task to re-create those values continuously in their behavior, facing the dilemmas and catastrophes of their own time. Each generation re-fights the crucial battles and either brings new vitality to the ideals or allows them to decay. Men and women who understand this truth and accept its implications will be well fitted to renew the moral order—and to renew their society as well.

If we are to successfully face the challenges of the future by striving for a continuously renewing and innovative society, we must also look to the past in an effort to understand who we are and what we stand for. According to the Greek author Cicero, anyone who does not look to history to guide them into the future is bound to repeat it.

Chapter 4

The Present: Understanding where we are

One of the things we can do, before charging off in all directions, is to understand where we are, how we got here, and what is happening on the larger scene. If we are to prepare successfully for the challenges facing us, we must do so with the knowledge that we are indeed asking the right questions.

We are in the midst of significant economic, social, cultural, political and environmental trends, which began in the 1980s. From an economic perspective, the major events of the last decade have been the reordering of global markets and a deepening of the debt crisis in much of the world. The forces that produced a restructured international economy were political and technological. One reason for the debt crisis is the consumption binge. Although helping many economies in the short run, the "enjoy now—pay later" behavior of individuals, businesses and government has seriously crippled our future capacity to invest in the technologies and facilities needed to remain competitive in the new global marketplace.

However, as important as economic development is, the most difficult of these trends to understand is not the economic, social, political or environmental but the one that has received the least amount of attention—culture.

At this point, I will attempt the difficult task of clearly defining what I understand "culture" and "development" to mean. In doing so I am reminded of the words of some wise person who said, "words don't have only one ultimate meaning—they mean what I want them to mean."

Culture

When I think of culture I think of every aspect of life: customs of food and dress, religion, gender relations, mentality, values, methods of communication including language and symbols, sociopolitical and economic behavior including know-how, technical knowledge, indigenous methods of making decisions and exercising power, methods of production and economic relations and so on. In my opinion, it is simply inclusive of all aspects of human activity.

Culture is the combination of the best thinking of any group of human beings at any given time as they try and adapt successfully to their natural and social environment while not destroying it. It is not something that just deals with the past history or traditions of a particular people. It is a dynamic process that is ever present and ever changing, embodying the values and beliefs of a particular group or region of a country. Hence, the importance of considering the concept of development in the context of "culture."

However, cultural analysis must not replace previous economic, social, environmental and political analyses; it should complement and amend them. Culture is understood here not as a collection of objects as a pastime for the privileged but as a vital process that underpins all aspects of a given community's life.

Culture is an all-inclusive process that, in the final analysis, includes development. For it is the idea of culture that gives both meaning and direction to economic activity, political decisions, community life, social conflict, technology and so on. It is, in fact, culture that gives development its reason for being and its goal. It is each people's culture that must decide what, for them, is a "good life." As I experience on a daily basis on Cape Breton Island, culture instills its rhythm on the life of a community and gives it direction. It is clearly better, therefore, not to speak of "the cultural aspects of development" as though culture were a more or less decorative accessory or "cultural development" as though it was only a question of culture of artistic creation. Culture in the broad sense is, properly speaking, the basis of "development." That raises the question: What do we mean by "development"?

Development

Development is a highly charged term that often lacks precision. It is paired with all sorts of qualifying adjectives: human, integral, self-reliant, alternative, local, upward, sustainable, social, economic…

Many people talk about trying to mobilize the indigenous culture as a "tool for development." Others are trying to replace the term "development" with the expression "a good life." Achieving the necessary conditions to lead "a good life" may be a less biased and more universal exercise than promoting the usual concept of development, as we in so-called "developed" countries have defined it.

I define development as overall human progress. Progress (development) results from advances in a combination of several dimensions of the human experience. The economic dimension is important but equally important are the political, technological, social, cultural, environmental, health and even the spiritual dimensions of human progress. As a matter of fact, all of these have an economic dimension.

I am most uncomfortable with the classic definition of economic development as the process of creating wealth through the mobilization of human, financial, capital, physical and natural resources to generate marketable goods and services. This definition leaves out everything that makes life worthwhile. After all, what we measure and count is reflective of what we value.

Sustainable Development

However, it must be understood that development is not the only reference for what is desirable. Since there are many cultures, there are also many ways of perceiving progress. There is little doubt a specifically Western cultural model has been the basis for most operations undertaken so far under the generic term "development."

The poverty of the so-called "third world countries" (as if they were on a separate planet) is not due to a historical backwardness that could be eliminated by the process of modernizing their economies. Rather, it is the result of a systematic process of exploitation of the "underdeveloped" countries by those in the "developed" countries. World economy is characterized by relationships of dependence between the "centers" and the "peripheries." This center-periphery schema is reproduced inside each country, including developed countries. As mentioned in the last chapter, much of the regional strategies employed in Canada over the past thirty years were based on this philosophy of development. Countries that are less developed economically must base their development on their needs. This means self-development based on collective self-reliance. What better way to guarantee any development that occurs will be able to sustain itself over the long term?

If we accept this as the ultimate goal for helping underdeveloped areas of the world, then what can developed countries do to help? It would seem logical to conclude the most useful thing we can do to help is to change the dominant sociopolitical and economic systems in our own respective countries.

There seems to be a growing body of evidence that people's movements, grassroots communities and ethnic minorities globally are asserting their dignity with increased strength and with a profound faith in their own capacities. In Canada, we have two exceptional examples.

Naomi Klein, the author of *No Logo*, wrote to strongly urge me to support the Canadian Center for Policy Alternatives (CCPA) located in Ottawa. According to her, the CCPA is countering the corporate-funded research in areas of public health care and social programs by encouraging public debate, thus attempting to shift the political debate in Canada one conversation at a time. She went on to say that only socially concerned citizens would fund the CCPA.

Another example is the Council of Canadians, a national group also headquartered in Ottawa. It is an organization of individuals trying to protect Canada from the negative aspects of policies included in international agreements like the North American Free Trade Agreement (NAFTA), which threaten Medicare, natural resources (especially water) and cultural programs in Canada. The Council of Canadians feels nothing is sacred or spared in these international agreements. The Council of Canadians is trying to reinvent democracy by attempting to get policies discussed and debated in public as opposed to having them decided in corporate boardrooms. I will return to this trend in the final chapter.

Chapter 5

The Future: Where do we want to go? How are we going to get there?

I was surprised to learn on my visits around the island, after returning from northern Ontario, that many Cape Bretoners had a common vision of what they wanted the economy (development?) of the island to look like. This vision was reinforced by what I read and heard in the local media. Although not articulated in a single statement, the vision many had for Cape Breton Island was to see the day when the island would be a more attractive place to live through fostering unification and trust in all members of the community. This would lead to progressive change and meet citizen expectations by identifying and pursing opportunities to enhance and improve the economic base and quality of life in a consultative and dynamic fashion. Because of recent provincial and municipal elections in the province we now have the opportunity to turn this vision into reality. We need comprehensive plans for each area considering itself “a community.” However, a comprehensive plan is not a detailed operational plan with five, ten or even twenty-five years added to it. The difference between a comprehensive community development plan and other forms of planning is time and scope. A comprehensive community development plan is inclusive of culture, history, traditions, social, environmental, health, education and economic needs of a community. It deals with long-term goals and aspirations in all areas. It goes to the heart of a community’s vision of its future and seeks to identify steps that must be taken into consideration to realize that vision.

Martin Luther King Jr. did not inspire his followers with a plan. He had a dream and he went on to describe the America he envisioned, where people appreciated differences and have respect for individuals due to the inherent dignity people have as human beings and not because of the color of their skin.

Why have we made so little progress in creating a comprehensive community-based development plan for Cape Breton Island? The reason we are in such difficulty seems simple. Our approach in the past can be described as addressing development issues with a “short term,” “quick fix” and “how to” mentality. The characteristics that will be required for the next decade are “long term,” “permanent solutions” and “clarity of purposes.” The last point is particularly important. Our purpose should relate to being independent and self-reliant as "Cape Bretoners." In the words of Father Moses M. Coady, the cofounder of the Antigonish Movement in Nova Scotia, we want to be "masters of our destiny."

The economic principles to guide us are simple; there are only four:

- Prevent unnecessary leakage of dollars from communities
- Support, encourage and invest in existing local business
- Promote start-up businesses
- Recruit new businesses that will help achieve local goals and reflect the values, talents and heritage of our culture.

These new ventures should be compatible with local values and aspirations. There is nothing wrong with establishing limits to growth. These principles of economic renewal are the fundamental elements; communities that look to their own resources, skills and unique opportunities will find they, themselves, hold the keys to their own economic engines.

There are requirements that can be considered the gas, or source of energy, to drive the engine of business opportunity:

- Access to capital

- Local business environment
- Infrastructure
- Human resources
- Quality of life.

Finally, all three levels of government need to set clear policies to guide future development in the province. These should be developed in meaningful consultation with a broad cross section of the public. The operative words are, "meaningful" consultation and "broad" cross section. What occurred in the past in the name of consultation, involvement or citizen participation has too often been anything but. There are at least five degrees of consultation possible when involving the public in decisions. Before discussing any of these, it is necessary to acknowledge what the public wants to be involved in. The public doesn't want to be involved in all or even in many decisions the government makes during day-to-day operations. The public wants to be involved, in a meaningful way, in important policies or major project developments. But who decides what is major? For the most part, politicians and/or bureaucrats can take a chance and make a judgment call and if they guess wrong the public will let them know. However, generally speaking, most politicians recognize that items of an economic nature, affecting a large number of jobs or having a serious impact on the environment, will be of interest to the public.

A more important question is: what constitutes meaningful involvement? The five degrees of involvement are:

- Informing the public about a course of action the sponsoring agency wishes to take
- Giving information to the public on a particular topic (often referred to as educating the public)
- Asking the public for their opinion, ideas or concerns on a course of action
- Inviting the public to participate in the decision-making process by presenting options before decisions are made
- Or, when the final decision is turned over to a group, committee or organization, that the public has confidence in it/them to represent its interests.

What many communities find most frustrating is that the government talks about public participation but doesn't define the degree of participation. There are times when the public would be satisfied with a lesser degree of participation as long as the government was forthright. When the government talks about consultation or participation, they seem to be referring to a fourth- or fifth-degree consultation—either sharing in a meaningful way in the decision-making process or having the authority to make a final decision. In fact, what is often proposed is a limited degree of consultation where the government wants to inform or educate (brainwash?) the public toward a preconceived conclusion.

Given that the public would welcome the opportunity to be more involved in meaningful discussions regarding development policies designed to guide them toward sustainable development, I would like to suggest some policy guidelines for discussion:

- Encourage local ownership and control of enterprises, when possible
- Attract business geared to local, permanent employment creation
- Provide support for healthy and satisfying work conditions which provide adequate income and opportunity to participate in the enterprise
- Establish economic initiatives that deliberately seek to create employment for those in the population who have found it difficult to obtain work (women, youth, older workers, disabled, single parents and other marginalized groups)
- Recognize the integral role played by non-monetary activity in the local economy
- Provide support and training in the use of technology
- Build local coordinating arrangements that forge new partnerships among diverse interests and broaden the base of participation in local enterprise development
- Create local investment/capital funds that are prepared to accept special arrangements and/or conditions to invest in the community
- Develop support mechanisms to provide advice and assistance to local enterprises at all stages of business development

- Finally, and not least of all, create a greater appreciation of the importance of cultural/heritage resources and their potential economic development value.

The most serious crisis Cape Breton faces is not the lack of development or economic activity on the island. The real crisis is the lack of trust people have in the three levels of government to provide the necessary leadership that would help the community face the challenges of the next decade. The problems we face were not created overnight, nor will they be solved in the immediate future. Politicians, bureaucrats, news media and the public must recognize that sustained economic progress does not conform to short-term deadlines—it unfolds over a period of years. Community leaders will need to be prepared to provide adequate resources to development organizations over the long run, whether or not results are forthcoming in the short run.

If we are to succeed in getting the community development we want, and use innovative thinking to address the challenges that face us, we must give the following elements serious consideration.

Emerging Global Trends

It is tempting to think the current economic slump is just part of a cycle—the pulp prices will rise and remain high, new industrial plants will hire hundreds of thousands of workers, new minerals will be discovered and new mines opened, call centers and tourism will solve problems, and life will resume its familiar pattern. This is not going to happen.

The winds of change are sweeping the world. We are not experiencing a cyclical recession but a fundamental restructuring—a great historical turning point comparable to the industrial revolution. Established industries are in decline; new ones are rising; global markets are opening while traditional protected markets are disappearing. Economic and technological shifts are changing all aspects of life—education, politics, social services, the way we navigate ships and plan houses, down to how we cook food.

In such turmoil, a failure to plan intelligently can have appalling long-term consequences. Even in the short term, an appropriate plan is essential. It is unfortunate that many federal and provincial departments do not require an economic strategy that is consistent with the overall objectives for that region of the province. Any comprehensive community development plan too rigid or too narrow and not oriented to the future should be blocked from funding. However, that is unlikely to become policy. It is too simple and makes too much common sense. As the English writer G. K. Chesterton once said, "the only problem with common sense is that it isn't very common."

In short, we must plan. A policy of drifting into the future by being reactive to existing economic conditions will only ensure our future will be less attractive than our present. Whether we like it or not, our planning process must take place in the context of sweeping, continuous global change and not only accommodate these changes but also anticipate them. The good news is, Cape Breton is in a great position to focus on comprehensive community development planning.

Contrary to popular belief, a time of crisis is not the time for action. What is required to face a crisis successfully is careful thought, before action. Yet the natural tendency is to want to act and to act decisively and immediately in a time of crisis. Because we are in a crisis on Cape Breton Island, it would be wise to try and figure out the right questions to ask. Certainly our past practices of having outside experts, consultants and bureaucrats from Halifax or Ottawa solve our problems have not borne much fruit. Our unemployment rate of 16 percent does not compare favorably with the national average, which is in the range of 8.7 percent. Cape Bretoners pay little attention to this figure because we know how misleading it is. The actual figures are hard to prove but most agree it is close to double the official figures. We have some time on our side but we can't put off the challenge indefinitely. We do not face major problems with crime, violence, drugs, insurrection, drought, overcrowding and the other miseries seen on the evening news. The serious problems we do face, like the pollution at the tar ponds in Sydney (supposedly the worst toxic waste site in Canada), can be a source of inspiration and empowerment if we approach them from a "new thinking" perspective. If proper research is done, these "problems" can be a source of future employment possibilities.

If we are to be successful in turning problems and crises into opportunities, we have to have the proper knowledge, understanding, skills and attitudes to make it happen. One of the most positive things we have going for us is people want a healthy local economy without changing local values or the social environment.

Past history and experience (as referred to in chapter two) should make us realize as "Cape Bretoners" that no one else is going to solve our problems—we will have to develop the economy. It will take our collective skill, courage and intelligence but in the end, we may find we are in a better situation than the island has seen in generations. Perhaps the immortal Pogo had it right: "We are surrounded by insurmountable opportunities."

The first step in the turnaround is the understanding that "if it is to be, it is up to me." We need to do community-based economic development; our own efforts are the only major resource that remains available. The second step is an accurate, unflinching analysis of our situation. The third step is an overall action plan.

Comprehensive community planning for community-based development, whether or not it is on Cape Breton Island, encompasses all three steps. Too often the strategic planning process becomes mired in analysis, going over and over the same broad issues in the same general terms. The goal is to move through the first two steps as quickly as possible and concentrate efforts on achieving the specific objectives set forth in the action plan.

The Old Economy

Traditionally our local community has depended on:

- Two large industrial sectors—coal and steel
- Importation of finished products
- Exportation of raw or semi-processed materials from rural areas of the island (forestry, and fishing products) to pay for the above
- Financing development of natural resources through the importation of capital.

The results from these actions have been:

- Costly subsidization of certain uneconomic industries
- "Branch-plant economy"
- Little integration of resource industries with the rest of the economy
- Manufacturing that must be protected because of the absence of the "economy scale."

However, "the times they are a-changing" and our resources can no longer fill those roles. They are not as valuable as they once were because:

- Developing nations are a cheaper source
- Certain materials are being replaced by new technology (for example, copper by fiber optics)
- They are rapidly becoming less competitive due to globalization

There have been significant changes in the world economy the last couple of years. In order to understand what some of these changes are, it may be worthwhile to look at the characteristics of the old or traditional economy. For example, many people (economists, academics, business people and bureaucrats) schooled in the old economy—or, more precisely, the old way of thinking—describe the economy almost entirely in terms of sales, profits and investments. They are used to describing the economy in terms of companies (and not people) with the following characteristics:

- Medium to large size
- Vertically integrated industries
- Own the raw material
- Own the capital
- Own the labor (relied on physical strength)
- Own the transportation systems to move things to market
- Self marketing, promotion and selling
- Resistant to change.

The large companies or corporations are also characterized by:

- Paying the lowest taxes possible
- Investing little in education and job training
- Keeping UIC (now Employment Insurance) and Workers Compensation down
- Avoiding unions, if possible
- Delaying or not enforcing environmental, health and safety standards
- Perceiving the government as the enemy
- Getting involved at the final stages of production cycle.

For example the Dominion Steel and Coal Company, in Sydney, Nova Scotia was the second largest employer in Canada in the 1950s and had a number of the characteristics described above.

The New Economy

There is a new approach or different attitude toward what the new economy is. If you ask a person "on the street" to describe the purpose of economic activity, the most common response will be: "to support and improve the lives of people." Business and government efforts to improve business vitality are the means to that end. Quality of life, income security and, if possible, meaningful, useful, productive jobs are what matter. But as mentioned earlier, jobs are a means to an end and not simply an end in themselves. So the new economy is characterized by:

- Multinational corporations
- Internationally integrated
- Materials, capital and labor gathered worldwide
- Contract "research and development" (R & D) studies
- Contract marketing, promotion and selling
- Development of management structures that encourage change
- Big money is not made at the end of the production cycle but is invested in research and development (R & D), which in turn provides capital creation for new products and services.

Other characteristics of the new economy are:

- Human labor replaced by technology
- Money/jobs at the beginning of the production cycle
- Research, ingenuity and risk capital creating new products and services
- Create entirely new market demand
- "Competitive"
- Trying to figure out what makes an economy "tick"
- People are the most important factor
- Government as a partner responsible for building the basic foundations, policy and infrastructure of the economy.

The Future: Where do we want to go?
How are we going to get there?

There are five factors essential to a strong local economy in this time of globalization:

- Adaptable workforce—development of people
- Long-term capital investment—invest in and maintain industrial infrastructure
- Technology and the latest management techniques—so people are in a continuous learning/training cycle
- Government to foster new and developing business—a balance between large and small business development
- Spirit of progress, entrepreneurship and a vision of the future.

Surveys conducted by the Corporation for Enterprise Development with Mt. Auburn Associates and the Institute on Taxation and Economic Policy in Washington, D.C., with Fortune 500 companies show key factors when locating new industries in a particular location are:

- Infrastructure
- Educated workforce and effective training programs
- Coherent environmental regulations.

Their surveys also show other keys to success are:

- Innovation
- Flexibility
- Resilience

- Adaptability

Strategic Directions for the New Economy

While it is true to say the new economy is a knowledge economy, this does not go far enough. We need new and relevant skills. Lack of knowledge also hampers entrepreneurs. According to a Canadian economist Diane Cohen, the most important wealth-creating instrument is the imagination. It allows the entrepreneur to see opportunities and imagine ways to meet them. But the imagination feeds on knowledge. In the information economy, learning never stops; the objective is not paper certification but essential skills and understanding. We must keep our children in school and demand school programs enrich their lives and prepare them for a meaningful life, as well as for a new economy. We need a powerful program of adult education to upgrade the skills and knowledge of the people who already live here.

It can be done. A significant advantage is our lifestyle. The new economy requires adaptable, multi-skilled people, who fit the lifestyle of this area. This tradition of multi-skilled and independent lifestyles on Cape Breton Island is a solid foundation for entrepreneurship.

The new world economy remains open to old industries with fresh ideas. The industries of the old economy will not disappear. Fewer people will be employed in them, even though their output will increase. Old industries will survive by embracing new-economy values like quality, service, design, innovation, marketing, customization and decentralization.

We should encourage our traditional industries to use newer production and management approaches—automating, producing efficiently, marketing aggressively, adding value and creating new products. We should also look for new economic activities developed without traditional industries; these tools are products that can be exported. We should see our competitors as our potential allies. For example, there has been an agreement that Nova Scotia will provide specialized training for the agriculture industry in Atlantic Canada while Prince Edward Island will provide a police academy and veterinary training in the region. These kinds of partnerships and joint ventures in private industry and government are the wave of the future—this way both parties win.

No community is an island unto itself; Cape Breton's economic strategy must be consistent with and complement a regional strategy for the six counties of eastern Nova Scotia. Citizens at large should play a key role in helping develop such a strategy in order to ensure it is consistent with their understanding of the new economy while respecting their values.

Designing a Community-Based Planning Process

Education is a leading out process, not a pouring in of information, data or knowledge. Also, designing a community planning process is both an art and a science. There are a number of components which constitute our regional community and a number of different kinds of "publics" that exist that will need to be meaningfully involved in the planning process.

Independent from the need to have a certain share in the benefits society bestows, there is, in most citizens, a desire to take part in the decision-making process. They are no longer content to accept what others believe is good for them. Unfortunately, there has not been a strong tradition of involving people, at least not in a meaningful way, in the decision-making process and in the management of our (their) resources.

We know what has to happen to change the situation. We lack the political will and the leadership required to do the job. Top-down planning has proven ineffective at addressing the community's long-term needs. Community-based planning is possible and is the only real hope for substantial change in the way communities are managed or run. Much of the outside "expert" advice addressing long-standing social, economic or human problems has not stood the test of time or brought about the desired changes. It remains to communities to try innovative approaches to the old problems. More than anything, this requires a new way of thinking about the challenges facing communities and how they can be successfully addressed.

Chapter 6

Can We Measure Progress Toward Quality of Life?

How are we going to know if we are on the right road for achieving the good life?

This chapter is intended to make a case for creating new methods for measuring progress as it relates to well-being and sustainable development on a societal level. I will attempt to answer the question: Can we measure real progress as it relates to quality of life in the affirmative. The old measures of measuring progress no longer work; they are based on traditional accounting systems that are obsolete because they only measure growth in strictly economic terms. The result is the old measures often lead to incorrect goals. What thinking person would hold that growth, per se, is a value worth living for?

It is hard to imagine anyone who does not want economic security and less poverty. Who does not want to live in a peaceful and safe society without crime? Most people value a clean environment with healthy forests, soils, lakes and oceans. We all want and need good health, strong communities and time to relax and develop our potential as human beings.

Why then do we not see policies that promote these very outcomes? Why have we not ordered our policies and priorities in accord with our shared values and human needs? Why have we been unable to create the kind of society we genuinely want to inhabit?

One reason is, we have been unwilling, for whatever reason, to hold our community leaders and politicians accountable for reflecting the values and beliefs we hold close. Maybe it is time for more of us "common folk" to consider taking on leadership positions rather than leaving it to the "experts." Certainly, we couldn't do worse than many leaders. Additionally, we have been completely hooked on the illusion that equates economic growth with well-being and prosperity. This was not the intention of those who created the GDP. Simon Kuznets, its principal architect, warned forty years ago:

"The welfare of a nation can scarcely be inferred from a measurement of national income…Goals for 'more' growth should specify of what and for what." [1]

In other words, we are getting the wrong message from our current measures of progress, which are based primarily on economic growth statistics as measured by changes in production and how much they cost. We, as a society, have measured progress in strictly materialistic terms for far too long. The more we produce, the better off we are. That measure is called the Gross Domestic Product (GDP)—it simply adds the total quantity of goods and services produced and the total amount of money earned and spent.

We should ask: Were the GDP statistics ever meant to be used as a measure of progress, as they are today? Think about the fact that activities that degrade our quality of life—like crime, pollution and addictive gambling—all make the economy grow. The more we deplete our natural resources through fishing and forestry, the more the economy grows. We don't assign a value to our natural capital and therefore count its depreciation as a gain. It's like the federal and provincial governments selling assets of the coal mines and steel plant on Cape Breton Island in 2001 and counting the revenue as profit.

In Canada, we have been enamored with the dynamic American economy and rapid growth rates through the 1990s. We do not ask, as Kuznets counsels: What is driving that growth?

Some of the fastest-growing sectors of the American economy are:

- Corrections and imprisonment, at an annual growth rate of 6.2 percent per year throughout the 1990s; one in every 150 Americans is now behind bars, the highest rate in the world compared to one in 900 Canadians and one in 1,600 Nova Scotians.
- The O. J. Simpson trial alone added $200 million
- The Oklahoma City explosion and Littleton massacre fueled the booming U.S. security industry, which now adds $40 billion a year
- Gambling is a $50-billion-a-year business
- Divorce adds $20 billion a year
- Car crashes add another $57 billion.
- Diet and weight-loss industries add $32 billion a year
- Obesity-related health problems add another $50 billion, while at the same time 20 million people in the world, mostly children, die every year from hunger and malnutrition.

If we take a few moments, we would realize toxic pollution, sickness, stress and war all make an economy grow. The *Exxon Valdez* contributed more to the Alaskan economy by spilling its oil than if it had delivered the oil safely to port, because the cleanup costs, lawsuits and media coverage added to the growth statistics. The Yugoslav War stimulated the economies of NATO countries to the tune of $60 million a day and economies will benefit even more by rebuilding what has been destroyed. The amount of money spent on security and the war on terrorism after September

11, 2001, not only by the U.S., but by other countries as well, is certainly in the billions of dollars.

When we think about what is driving our growth in this context, we realize our growth statistics make no distinction between economic activity that contributes to well-being and that which causes harm. Growth is simply a quantitative increase in the physical scale of the economy and it tells us nothing about our actual well-being.

It is ironic that while we are so busy keeping track of everything we spend money on, we assign no economic value to vital unpaid activities that contribute to well-being. Citizenship and voluntary community service, which constitute the backbone of a civil society, are not counted or valued in the measures of progress because money isn't exchanged. If we did measure them, we would know volunteer services to the elderly, sick, disabled, children and other vulnerable groups have declined throughout Canada during the 1990s. At the same time, government has cut social services, leading to cumulative 30 percent erosion in the social safety net.

Even though household work and raising children are more essential to the basic quality of life than much of the work done in offices, factories and stores, they hold no value within the GDP. On the other hand, every additional lawyer, broker and advertising executive is counted as a contribution. We value the booming child care industry as the fourth fastest-growing industry in the country but we do not count unpaid child care. As a result, it seems to go unnoticed that parents are spending less time with their children than ever before. Is this a sign of progress?

If the GDP counted voluntary and household work, we would see they add $325 billion a year to the Canadian economy. If we measured the household—not just as a source of consumption, as taught in economic textbooks, but as a productive economic unit—we would discover that total paid and unpaid work has steadily increased. In 1900, a single-earner, male, breadwinner worked a 59-hour week in Canada, while a full-time, female, homemaker put in an average 56-hour week of household work, for a total household workweek of 115 hours. Today the average Canadian couple puts in 79 hours of paid work and 56 hours of unpaid household work a week, for a total household workweek of 135 hours.

The extra paid hours fuel economic growth and are counted as progress, while the loss of "precious free time" is invisible and unvalued in the measures of progress. Aristotle recognized 2,400 years ago that leisure was a prerequisite for contemplation, informed discussion, participation in political life and genuine freedom. It is also essential for relaxation and health, for spiritual practice and for a decent quality of life.

What happens if we do not count on monetary and nonmaterial assets? In effect, we systematically discount and devalue them. What we don't measure and value in our central accounting mechanism will be effectively sidelined in the policy arena. We often pay pious public homage to environmental quality and to social and spiritual values. If we count their degradation as progress in our growth measures and do not count their preservation or improvement as assets, we continue to send misleading signals to policy makers and the public. The result will blunt effective remedial action and distort policy priorities.

Working longer hours makes the economy grow. As is becoming more evident, economies can grow while increasing in inequality and poverty. Until we explicitly assign economic value to free time, voluntary community service, parental time with children and natural resource wealth, they will never receive adequate attention on the public policy agenda.

Similarly, until we assign an explicit value to equity in our growth measures, we will continue to give little policy attention to the fact that in Nova Scotia the poorest 40 percent of households have lost 20 percent of their real income after taxes and transfers since 1990.

The obsession with economic growth and its confusion with quality of life have led us down a dangerous and self-destructive path. It is doubtful we will leave our children a better legacy until we stop gauging our well-being and prosperity by how fast the economy is growing and until we stop misusing the GDP as a measure of progress. It is important to remember when reading the following quote from Robert Kennedy, just before he was assassinated, that the only difference between the Gross Domestic Product (GDP) and the Gross National Product (GNP) is the fact that the GDP does not include the income to residents from investments abroad.

"Too much and too long, we seem to have surrendered community excellence and community values in the mere accumulation of material things. The Gross National Product (GNP) includes air pollution and advertising for cigarettes and ambulances to clear our highways of carnage. It counts special locks for our doors and jails for the people who break them. The GNP includes the destruction of the redwoods and the death of Lake Superior. It grows with the production of napalm and missiles and nuclear warheads." [2]

If the GNP includes all of this, there is much it does not comprehend. It does not allow for the health of our families, the quality of their education or the joy of their play. It is indifferent to the decency of our factories and the safety of our streets. It does not include the beauty of our poetry or the strength of our marriages or the intelligence of our public debate or the integrity of our public officials. The GNP measures neither our wit nor our courage, neither our wisdom nor our learning, neither our compassion nor our devotion to our country. It measures everything, in short, except that which makes life worthwhile. Ralph Nader once said, "You contribute to the GNP when you run your car into someone else's; your contribution is still greater if you hurt the people inside."

What is urgently—indeed, desperately—needed are measures of well-being, prosperity and progress that explicitly value the nonmaterial assets that are the true basis of wealth, including the strength of communities, free time, the quality of environment, the health of natural resources and concern for others. The means to do so exist.

In fact, tremendous progress has been made in the last twenty years in natural resource accounting and in developing good social indicators, time-use surveys, environmental quality measures and other means of assessing well-being and quality of life. We are now capable of measuring progress in a better way that accords itself with our shared values and lets us know we are moving toward the society we want to create.

Fortunately, considerable headway has been made in recent years in developing more comprehensive measures of progress that integrate social, environmental and economic factors. One such effort was the Genuine Progress Index (GPI), developed by Americans Cobb, Halstead and Rowe in 1995, which measured twenty-six variables. In response, four hundred leading economists, including Nobel Prize winners wrote:

"The signatories agree that since the GNP/GDP measures only the quantity of market activity without accounting for the social and ecological costs involved—it is both inadequate and misleading as a measure of true prosperity.

Policy makers, economists, the media and international agencies should cease using the GNP/GDP as a measure of progress and publicly acknowledge its shortcomings." [3]

New indicators of progress are urgently needed that include the presently un-priced value of natural and social capital in addition to the value of conventionally measured economic production. The GPI is an important step in this direction.

GPI Atlantic is a nonprofit research society dedicated to creating a GPI for Nova Scotia and Atlantic Canada. There is at present a project in Kings County, Nova Scotia and in the community of Glace Bay on Cape Breton Island, which are constructing a GPI for their communities, integrating social and environmental factors into economic accounts. They are examining twenty social, economic and environmental indicators, selected in consultation with Statistics Canada, to get a truer picture of social well-being and prosperity and to determine whether progress in the region is sustainable over time. It is designed as a practical, policy-relevant tool that is easy to maintain and replicate and that can accurately measure sustainable development. It will provide information to policy makers about issues that are currently hidden and even invisible in market statistics.

The social and spiritual values and the quality of our environment, which are vital to our well-being and prosperity, have been sidelined when measuring progress.

The Nova Scotia GPI will not be a rigid final product but will develop with improvements in valuation methods, additional indicators and new data sources. We have an opportunity in Nova Scotia to take the lead in creating a new economy for the twenty-first century that will genuinely reflect the social, spiritual, environmental and human values of our society.

Components of the Nova Scotia GPI which are not currently measured by the GDP include:

- The value of voluntary work, unpaid housework and child-care
- Trends in income distribution
- Trends in leisure time
- A livelihood security index, including the cost of underemployment and the value of unpaid overtime
- The cost of crime
- Natural resource accounts for forestry, soil, agriculture, subsoil assets and wildlife
- Greenhouse gas emissions
- Air and water quality and costs of pollution
- An ecological footprint analysis
- A transportation cost analysis
- Valuations of durability
- Trends in debt loads
- Trends in health care and educational quality.

Beginning in July 1998, data was released on each of these components, as they became available. When each of the components was complete, the information was integrated with existing market statistics to construct an overall index of sustainable development for the province—the GPI.

The index goes up as society becomes more equal, if we have more free time and our quality of life is improving. It counts health, educational attainment and economic security. It attempts, in short, to measure "that which makes life worthwhile." It is common-sense economics that corresponds with the realities of our daily lives as we experience them.

Unlike the GDP, the GPI distinguishes economic activities that produce benefit from those that cause harm. Having a more peaceful society may actually show up as a disadvantage in the GDP and growth statistics.

Although the final results will not be released for some time, GPI Atlantic has already found that crime costs Nova Scotians $1.2 billion a year, or $3,500 per household, including $312 million in victim losses; $258 million in public spending on prisons, police and courts; and $46 million in home-security expenses. Nova Scotian households pay $800 more a year due to in-store retail theft and business crime prevention costs and $200 more per household in higher insurance premiums due to insurance fraud. [4]

Canadians are three times as likely to be victims of crime as their parents were a generation ago. According to the GPI, this is not a sign of progress, even though the economy may grow as a result. GPI Atlantic found if crime was still at 1962 levels, Nova Scotians would be saving about $750 million a year or $2,200 per household.

The GPI takes a similar approach to road accidents, toxic pollution and greenhouse gas emissions, which are seen as costs rather than benefits. Like crime and resource depletion, they are areas of the economy where more growth is clearly not desirable.

By incorporating "external" costs directly into the economic accounting structure, the "full cost accounting" mechanisms in the GPI can also help policy makers identify investments that produce lower social and environmental costs to society. Gambling, clear-cutting and other growth industries might receive less government support if social costs were counted and sustainable practices might receive more encouragement.

For example, GPI Atlantic recently found that a 10 percent shift from truck to rail freight would save Nova Scotia taxpayers $11 million a year when the costs of greenhouse gas emissions, road accidents and road maintenance costs were included. Recently Nova Scotia refused a request to subsidize a 7.2-mile rail spur to Georgia Pacific's Melford gypsum mine site on Cape Breton Island, even though the current users would have likely agreed to pay a third of the cost as long as the mining company paid for another third. However, Transport 2000's John Pierce noted the province spent $1.4 million to upgrade the Trans-Canada Highway between Melford and Port Hawkesbury to accommodate gypsum trucks. The additional truck traffic through town brought new calls for a bypass around Port Hawkesbury, a project that could cost an additional $14 million. Consequently, Rail America may close the railway on Cape Breton Island, partially due to this decision. Rail America enjoyed $17 million in profits in the last fiscal year. Over 300 jobs, with the 18 present users of the railroad, are threatened if the line is discontinued.

Telecommuting (working at home) two days per week would save $2,200 annually per employee when travel time, fuel, parking, accident, air pollution and other environmental and social costs are included.

The GPI approach contrasts sharply with conventional accounting methods, which value the contribution that commuting makes to economic growth. Canadians currently spend $102 billion a year on their cars, $11 billion more on highways, $500 million on car advertisements and billions more on hospitals, police, courts and funeral costs for the 3,000 killed and 25,000 seriously injured in car crashes every year.

This spending currently counts as progress and contributes to assessments of consumer confidence. By contrast, carpooling may slow GDP growth even though it produces major savings in fuel costs and avoids environmental and social damages. Full cost-benefit accounting methods would lend more support to taxation policies and subsidy incentives that support mass transit alternatives and other more sustainable practices.

An example of a more sustainable practice is in Lake Ainslie. Their local development association is exploring the concept of a funeral cooperative. At present, funerals on Cape Breton Island cost $6,500 to $10,000. A funeral co-op from mainland Nova Scotia offers a first class but basic funeral for an all-inclusive price of $2,800. If the person is under 12 years of age, there is no cost to the family. Lake Ainslie can be accused of lowering the Canadian GDP/GNP by taking $3,700 out of the local economy or looked at in terms of a funeral cooperative generating $3,700 for a family so they can use the extra money to improve their quality of life or at least lessen the burden of burial costs.

The cost of holding on to the illusion "more is better" is frightening. Scientists recognize the only biological organism that has unlimited growth as its dogma is the cancer cell, the apparent model for our conventional economic theory. By contrast, the natural world thrives on balance and equilibrium and recognizes inherent limits to growth. The cancer analogy is apt—the path of limitless growth is profoundly self-destructive. No matter how many cars we have in the driveway or how many possessions we accumulate, the environment will not tolerate the growth illusion even if we fail to see through it.

Valuing both natural resources and time provides an accounting framework that recognizes inherent limits to economic activity and values balance and equilibrium. In the GPI, natural resources are valued as finite capital stocks, subject to depreciation like produced capital. Genuine progress is measured by the ability to live off the income, or services, produced by our resources without depleting the capital stock that is the basis of wealth for our children and ourselves.

The GPI acknowledges the full range of ecological and social services provided by these resources. The GPI Forest Account, for example, counts not only timber production, but also the value of forests in protecting watersheds, habitat and biodiversity; guarding against soil erosion; regulating climate and sequestering carbon; and providing for recreation and spiritual enjoyment. Healthy soils and the maintenance of multi-species, multi-aged forests in turn provide multiple economic benefits by enhancing timber productivity, increasing the economic value of forest products, protecting against fire, disease and insects; and supporting the burgeoning ecotourism industry.

The massive unemployment created by the collapse of the Atlantic ground fishery punctured the conventional illusion that jobs and environmental conservation are in conflict. Failure to protect and conserve a valuable natural resource resulted in the loss of 40,000 fishery jobs in the region.

Can We Measure Progress Toward Quality of Life?

We now understand that soil erosion threatens food security and that valuing and protecting resource wealth is essential to protecting the human economy.

Like natural resources, time is also finite and similarly limits economic activity. We all have 24 hours a day and a limited life span. How we pass that time and how we balance our paid and unpaid work, our voluntary service and our free time, are measures of our well-being, quality of life and contribution to society. The GPI uses time-use surveys to measure and value time over a 24-hour period and to assess the balance between its alternative uses. Measuring time as time, rather than as money, also cuts through the myth of limitless growth.

What happens when we start valuing time? The policy implications are profound. For example, GPI Atlantic found that Nova Scotians have the highest rate of volunteer activity in the country, giving 134 million hours a year, the equivalent of 81,000 jobs, or $1.9 billion in services, equal to 10 percent of our GDP—a reservoir of generosity completely invisible in our conventional accounts. Unmeasured and unvalued, the volunteer sector has not received the support it needs to do its work well.

Longer work hours due to downsizing and declining real incomes have squeezed volunteer time, producing a steady decline of 7.2 percent in voluntary service hours over the past ten years. For the first time, claims by a Canadian finance minister that volunteers could compensate for government service cuts have been disproved. Without tracking the unpaid volunteer sector, such government statements can never be tested.

Measuring unpaid household work shines the spotlight on the time stress of working parents struggling to juggle job and household responsibilities and on the need for family-friendly work arrangements and flexible work hours. The modern workplace has not yet adjusted to the reality that women have doubled their rate of participation in the paid workforce. Working mothers put in an average of 11 hours a day of paid and unpaid work on weekdays and over 15 hours of unpaid work on weekends. According to Statistics Canada, the average working mother today puts in a 75-hour workweek.

Measuring housework also raises important pay equity issues. Work traditionally performed by women in the household and regarded as free has been devalued in the market economy, resulting in significant gender pay inequities. Although it is an important investment in our human capital and it requires vital skills and continuous alertness, child care workers in Nova Scotia only earn an average of $7.58 an hour.

GPI Atlantic found that single mothers dependent on the household economy put in an average of 50 hours a week of productive household work. If it were replaced for pay in the market economy, this work would be worth $450 a week. Because it is invisible and unvalued, 70 percent of single mothers in Nova Scotia live below the low-income cutoff. It makes one wonder if unpaid household work is the major cause of poverty in the province. Some refer to this lack of support for families as child poverty. There is no such thing as child poverty. There are homeless children but this is certainly the exception in most developed countries. Generally speaking, families are poor. Parents are poor. Single mothers or fathers are poor. Most children are poor because they are part of a poor household. They are not independently poor, isolated from the rest of the family. From the GPI perspective, social supports for single mothers are not "welfare" any more than taxpayer subsidies for job creation in the market economy are "welfare." They are seen, instead, as essential social infrastructure for the household economy.

Millions of Americans have been left behind by the growth spurt in their country too. The U.S. Census Bureau reports that income inequality has risen dramatically since 1968: by 18 percent for all U.S. households and by over 23 percent for families. The richest 1 percent of American households now owns 40 percent of the national wealth, while the net worth of middle class families has fallen steadily through the 1990s due to rising indebtedness. Is this progress?

In 1989, the Canadian House of Commons unanimously vowed to eliminate child poverty by the year 2000. Since 1989 child poverty has increased by 47 percent. In other words, there is no guarantee the tide of economic growth lifts all boats and the evidence indicates the opposite is frequently the case.

For this reason, the GPI explicitly values increased equity and job security as benchmarks of genuine progress. Indeed, Statistics Canada recently recognized concern for equity is inherent in any measure of sustainable development. Once limits to growth are accepted, the issue is fair distribution rather than increased production. If global population consumed resources at the Canadian level, we would require four additional planets.

Statistics Canada points to a growing polarization of hours as the main cause of increased earnings inequality. The growth of insecure, temporary and marginal employment—the engine of employment growth in the 1990s—means more Canadians cannot get the work hours they need to support themselves. At the same time, due to downsizing and declining real incomes, more Canadians are working longer hours.

By counting underemployment and overwork as economic costs and giving explicit value to equity and free time, the GPI can point to a range of intelligent job creation strategies that are not dependent on more growth.

This doesn't mean we shouldn't anticipate growth of any kind. Some types of economic growth clearly enhance well-being, increase equity and protect the environment. There is vital work to be done in our society—raising children, caring for those in need, restoring forests, providing adequate food and shelter, enhancing knowledge and understanding and strengthening communities. For example, the Lake Ainslie Development Association (LADA) is exploring the idea of letting the community create jobs by addressing unmet community needs and providing valuable work experience, in much the same way private industry receives government funding for creating jobs.

We won't shift our attention to the work that is needed if we fail to value our natural resources, voluntary service and child rearing and if we place no value on equity, free time and the health of our communities. We won't escape the materialist illusion that has trapped us, or even know whether we are really better off, if we continue to count costs like crime and pollution as benefits and if we measure well-being according to the GDP and economic growth statistics.

We can begin to fashion more self-reliant and self-sufficient forms of community economic development that provide an alternative to increasing reliance on the international market and puts our destiny in the hands of forces that are beyond our control. Knowing *more* is not the key to happiness and well-being; we can take back our future and perhaps even live a little more simply.

Even a casual observer of social trends will notice the large increase in the number of people reorganizing their work lives, often at substantial financial cost, to achieve a greater sense of consequence and satisfaction about what they do. Several American friends of mine, who are consultants with multinational corporations, tell me they have noticed a new trend in the past few years. Senior executives are looking for greater meaning in their working life and in their relationships with their "significant other." It is evidently not unusual for top corporations to send senior executives away for several weeks at a time to renew their spirit or well-being. Surprisingly, they are not expected to conduct business or solve corporate problems during these "retreats." Often one of the sessions involves their significant other to help ensure the health of their personal relationships. Two dear friends of mine, Dick and Marion Vittitow, from the Path Setters Institute of Research and Application for Social and Organizational Innovation in Santa Cruz, California, offer an annual program entitled, "Working with Greater Meaning in Life and Work." There is often a waiting list for participants. I am planning to bring them to Cape Breton Island next year to offer the program. It is encouraging that more people, especially senior executives, are looking for this type of experience.

Nova Scotia seems to be particularly fertile ground for this type of experiment with GPI; it has been just far enough removed from the materialist mainstream to preserve its community strength, spiritual values, quality of life and strong tradition of generous community service, more effectively than many parts of North America. The province has also experienced firsthand the collapse of a natural resource, the fishing industry. It has not generally been well served by conventional economic theory, thus creating a greater openness to alternatives.

Again, if I use our local development as an example: a few years ago, the LADA participated in a visioning workshop. We created a vision for what we wanted the community to be in the year 2020. Our vision statement is: "Lake Ainslie is economically, socially and environmentally sound."

We have before us the opportunity to get the question right. What kind of inheritance are we actually leaving our children? What can we do to leave this place stronger, more beautiful and more caring than we found it? How can we more accurately value our assets, remedy our weaknesses and measure that which makes life worthwhile?

By explicitly counting, measuring and valuing our social and environmental assets and integrating these into the economic accounts, GPI can help create the basis for genuine prosperity and well-being in this region and beyond. GPI proponents look forward to cooperating with a wide range of partners in helping forge the new economy of the next millennium.

The beginning of a millennium is a rare moment in history when a long-term practical vision can actually overpower our habitual short-term preoccupations. The time has never been better to contemplate the legacy we are leaving our children and the society we want to inhabit the new millennium. It is a moment that invites us to lay the foundations of a genuinely decent society for the sake of our children and all the world's inhabitants.

Chapter 7

Why jobs are not the answer

The following four chapters focus on four case studies, spanning a thirty-six-year period, that demonstrate why jobs are not the answer. What follows is a detailed description of four developmental processes that were designed and successfully conducted at the community level. What is interesting about the case histories is in each instance the approach was significantly different due to local circumstances. They differ in community context, time frame and issues. They share a common ground in their concern for the process by which individuals take control of their lives and how groups of people take responsibility for the socio-economic health of their communities. What did not change were the basic principles of community development—namely, starting where people are and not where someone else wants them to be, dealing initially with their agenda items and building on their knowledge of root causes of the local situation. At the same time, it was important to help them understand the impact of the global economy or national policy on their community and to take this impact and national policy into account when developing strategies to create meaningful change.

Case Study # 1 — Not for Charity but for Justice — Austin, Texas

Background

In the early 1960s, President Kennedy initiated five programs as part of the war on poverty established by the Economic Opportunity Act under the (OEO) in the Department of Labor of the United States. These programs included the Peace Corps (international), Volunteers in Service to America (VISTA—the national Peace Corps), the Job Corps, the Neighborhood Youth Corps (NYC) and a national day care program for preschoolers. Although all of the programs played an important role in the strategy to fight poverty, the NYC played a particularly critical role on the "home front" throughout the U.S. in the struggle for social justice.

The objective of the NYC program was to help young people from low-income families, between the ages of sixteen and twenty-one, by giving them jobs, paying them wages (the federal minimum wage of $1.25 at that time) and providing them with useful work experience through participation in state and community work training programs. The belief was their employability would increase or their education resumed or continued as a result of their participation in the program. Another benefit was that public agencies and private nonprofit organizations (other than political parties) could use the participants to provide services they otherwise could ill afford.

In 1965, I was hired by the board of directors of the Montopolis Community Center to direct the first NYC program in Austin, Texas. The Montopolis Community Center was a nondenominational, nonprofit corporation established for the development and improvement of the community and its people, without regard to nationality, race or religious belief. The geographic area served by this organization was known as the Montopolis area of Austin, the most impoverished area in Travis County and that region of the state. The area, with a population of approximately six thousand, was 80 percent Spanish-speaking residents and 20 percent African-American. The board of directors included professionals from Austin including the mayor, a state senator, state social, welfare and justice officials; senior representatives from the City of Austin Parks and Recreation Department and the University of Texas athletic department; a vice president of Capital National Bank; the owner and managers of local television and radio stations; the executive vice president of the Texas Restaurant Association; a Baptist pastor and a parish priest; owners of major businesses in the area; principals of local schools; and a representative group of eight local residents.

I was careful to watch and see how the eight local residents would participate in board meetings. I think without realizing it, I assumed they would play a minor role and were just there as "token" representatives of the community. Nothing was further from the truth. Although many of them did not have a strong formal education, they were chosen because of their strong individual characteristics and commitment to their community. The local parish priest, who initiated the project and was the first chairman of the board of directors, involved the entire community in carefully choosing a group of people representing both religious and ethnic culture in the neighborhood. He was also confident those selected would have the best interest of the community at heart. Other board members were careful not to dominate the meetings and made a point to seek out the opinion of local community representatives on issues under discussion. Board meetings were run with sufficient structure to get the work done but with enough informality so everyone participated easily. When the "locals" spoke, everyone listened intently and weighed their input carefully. Although the local residents only made up one third of the board, their influence went far beyond their numbers. It was due to the sense of "local ownership" by the board of directors and the trainees that made the program a success.

Selection Criteria

Before the program began, I negotiated an arrangement for the Montopolis NYC to be the first of its kind in the state to incorporate in-school and out-of-school trainees in the same program. The rationale was my belief that each group could positively influence the other if we were to create the proper environment for healthy exchanges. For in-school trainees (who worked sixteen hours a week), the NYC provided the opportunity to stay in school, giving them a better chance to get the type of job they wanted, hold it once they got it and earn more money in the future. For out-of-school trainees (who worked thirty-two hours a week), the NYC furnished the opportunity to resume school or improve their work habits, attitudes and skills through work experience so an employer would be more inclined to hire them when they completed the program.

The Trainees

We wanted to offer our target population of youth, those who had been neglected and pushed aside, the opportunity to gain the "self-respect" and a "feeling of belonging" that are musts for good citizenship. We knew we could make our program look well by selecting those most likely to succeed in the program. However, in consultation with the board of directors, our policy was to recruit the "hard core" cases—those youth who were disadvantaged in other ways, in addition to poverty. Once the policy was established, I singled out young people who were poor academic achievers, had poor attitudes toward work, were culturally deprived, had social and emotional adjustment problems and/or were physically or mentally handicapped.

There were six permanent gangs operating in the Montopolis area when the program began and I managed to recruit five gang leaders and members from all six gangs into the program. After all, I was of the belief that "leader" was the operative word, not "gang." I also obtained an exception to the national guidelines and recruited three young women who were high school graduates but could not obtain employment. All three had graduated with a major in secretarial science but, in fact, could not type twenty-five words a minute, let alone the forty they were supposedly qualified to type.

Within a few weeks we had sixty-seven young men and women (an almost equal number of each gender), forty-one in the in-school program and twenty-six in the out-of-school program. Many of these young adults came from problem or broken homes, some were on parole, others were drug addicts, some were divorced before they were twenty-one, others were single mothers and still others were victims of early marriages (eight were married before the age of sixteen).

The Program

The young adults received training as maintenance personnel, automotive mechanics, landscaping assistants, secretaries, day-care assistants, researchers (area survey workers) and recreational program supervisors. The program included a provision for the placement of trainees in regular jobs or for a referral to programs appropriate for their education or training at the expiration of their enrollment, unless they continued their education. We worked closely with the Texas State Employment Agency for further training and job placement. What was unique about our approach was the follow-up program set up to assist them once they received job placement.

In addition to individual counseling, I provided four hours of group counseling every week covering such topics as:

- History, tradition and ethnic cultures in the area
- Public speaking and the art of effective communication (listening)
- How to promote one's own mental health
- When and how to ask for help (counseling and/or therapy—individual, couples)
- Conflict with the law—why it happens and how to prevent it
- Leadership (gang/community)
- Drugs, narcotics, alcoholism
- Sociology: juvenile delinquency—causes and solutions
- Career life choices—how to make informed decisions
- Healthy relationships—how to establish and

maintain them
- Health and safety
- Banking, savings and credit
- Problem solving and decision making.

After lengthy discussions with senior officials in the police department, two police officers came out to present a program on police-youth relations. It was the first time either party met each other outside of a conflict situation. The officers came early, they let the "kids" play with their equipment (including their motorcycles) and they began the process of getting to know each other as people. The sergeant in charge convinced the trainees everything said was "off the record." He asked how many drove a vehicle. Almost everyone put up their hand. Then he asked how many had a driver's license. A half dozen put up their hand. The officers organized a driver's training and within a couple of months, everyone driving a vehicle had a driver's license. By the time the officers left the counseling session, the "kids" had become "young adults." Relations with the police department improved almost overnight.

I suggested the participants set up their own discipline committee with a mandate to develop a "code of conduct" and recommend disciplinary action. Although I retained the right to make a final decision, I never overruled the committee. However, I personally appeared before the committee on more than one occasion, pleading for them to give someone a second, third or in one case, a fourth chance. They were much harder on each other than I could ever be because they valued the program so much and didn't want anyone to jeopardize it.

One of our board members asked me if I thought any of our trainees would be interested in attending the symphony. My initial temptation was to say no but the more I thought about it, the more curious I became regarding their answer. I was surprised—they gave a resounding YES. The board member said he could get fifty tickets in the center of the concert hall. He arranged for tickets so all of the trainees would have several opportunities to go throughout the season.

However, there was a problem. The young people wanted to go in uniform—to go in common dress apparel, so they could be easily identified as the Montopolis NYC. I was dead against any talk about a uniform. I did not want any military nuances slipping into the program or for them to be confused in the minds of the public with the federal job corps who did have uniforms. Nevertheless, they persisted, asking inane questions like: What was blocking me from having an open mind to this question? Why was I not willing to look at all of the alternatives before making up my mind? What would it take to change my mind? I was obviously getting frustrated. Then they informed me that some of their decision-making and problem-solving sessions were hitting home and that's where these "inane" questions came from. I finally agreed to the uniforms if they met what I thought were almost impossible conditions. 1.) They could not look like uniforms. 2.) They would have to pay for the uniforms themselves. 3.) The uniforms had to be something they could use once they left the program.

In one meeting, they not only met all of the conditions but also came up with a logo and motto to go on the uniforms. They would consist of white blouses and grey skirts for the women and white shirts and grey dress pants for the men. They went to a quality clothing store, told them about the NYC and negotiated the purchase of the uniforms at cost. There would be a red badge sewn on both shoulders, consisting of the word Montopolis and the initials NYC in the center surrounded by a motto they adopted: "Not for Charity but for Justice." (How many board of directors of multinational corporations would have made so many good decisions in such a short time?) They attended the Austin Symphony, in uniform, and were introduced at intermission to a standing ovation. They enjoyed the music and were never prouder—nor was I.

Within a few months of the origination of the MNYC, an Austin newspaper began hounding me to allow them to do a major "spread" on the program. They were particularly interested in the fact that I was a Canadian and wanted to focus the story on how I managed to come from the east coast of Canada to work in the war on poverty. I managed to put them off for several more months until I was confident our initial successes were not temporary and we had enough "good news" to withstand any scrutiny. I insisted on two conditions: the reporter must come with an accomplished photographer and they must focus the story on the trainees. The reporter wrote a wonderful article telling the stories of many of the young people. He included several full pages of close-up photographs showing the faces that really told the story without any commentary. The only reference to me was my name and title—both of which they got wrong.

Following the story I got a call from the principal of an exclusive private Anglican boarding school just outside Austin. He wanted to have his students exposed to the "other side of life"—"to learn what it was like to grow up poor." I had some serious reservations if any good could come from such an exchange. However, after several visits by the principal (during which we became friends), I finally agreed to have a busload of his students visit our program. The exchange proved mutually beneficial. It turned out that young people, even from quite different cultural, social and economic environments, had more in common with each other than they had differences. The boarding school students invited the NYC youth to a barbecue at their school. Thus began regular exchange visits which were continuing when I left the program over a year later.

As mentioned earlier, the chairman of the board of directors was the local Catholic priest; he was also a former World-War-II pilot. He went to Chicago and obtained an old U.S. Navy bus, loaded it with donated clothes and furniture, attached an old '58 Ford to the back with a tow bar and drove it back to Austin. The bus was in terrible shape—it needed a motor job (it burned almost as much oil as gas) and serious body repairs. The young men in the automotive repair program wanted to do the motor and paint the bus in time for their first field trip—to the Houston Astrodome, which had just been built and where the first bullfight ever held in the U.S. was scheduled. I personally would not agree to go on the trip because I was against bullfighting as a sport but agreed they could take the field trip if it meant that much to them. During the time they were making the repairs to the bus they would not allow me (even though I thought I had built up a lot of trust with them) or any member of the staff or board near the building where the repairs were being done. They simply insisted I trust them and they would have a surprise on the appointed day. They certainly did. They did a fine job on the motor but the paint job was even more spectacular. They had painted the old dark blue Navy bus completely white, there was a huge green dragon on each side with bright red and yellow flames shooting around the front of the bus, joining the flames from the dragon on the other side. It was a sight to behold. They swore every vehicle between Austin and Houston blew their horn in recognition of their fine art work. They also said they didn't have any trouble finding it in the parking lot after the bullfight.

The Result

Within three months of the inception of the MNYC, the three high school graduates were typing sixty words a minute without an error (our supervisor would not allow correction fluid on the premises) and had obtained permanent placements—one in a law office, one in a health facility and the third went to work for IBM. Within six months, all six gangs had disappeared. Loan-sharking was cut in half, police/youth conflicts almost disappeared, the city recreation department was hiring our graduates and day-care assistants received official certification and placement in a local day-care center. The local golf course and a landscaping company hired all the landscape assistants we could provide. Service stations and automotive repair shops hired people because of the MNYC trainees' reputation for honesty and reliability.

The Neighborhood Youth Corps was part of a nationwide program aimed at providing individuals an opportunity to develop their capabilities and participate in the economic and social working of their community. For most of the young adults, the importance of the NYC went beyond money and work. As important as the money and work experience was, it was really the improvement in self-confidence and self-esteem that made the difference. Their attendance at the Austin Symphony, designing and paying for their own uniforms, the positive newspaper coverage, their trip to Houston on "their" bus and the friends they made with students from the exclusive private school, had more to do with their success than the upgrading and training they received. I am confident the graduates left the program not only better prepared for the work world but also better prepared to face the challenges of life.

A few years ago, I had to phone the local Montopolis parish to obtain a copy of my daughter's baptismal certificate, she was getting married. Because I knew funding for the NYC had eventually been phased out, I took the opportunity to inquire about what had happened since I left and if the program had any lasting results. I was surprised to learn that the program had been so successful, the city of Austin had taken over many of the social and recreation programs and the Montopolis Community Center was still functioning at full capacity. I think many of the programs offered at the center continued all these years because of the sense of ownership by the community.

Chapter 8

Case Study # 2 — Management Planning in a Tense Environment— Newfoundland and Labrador, Canada

Background

In the mid 1960s, the federal government of Canada and the provincial government of Newfoundland decided to create a new national park in western Newfoundland. The Newfoundland government proceeded to expropriate the required land including a dozen small communities. By 1970, control of the land had been turned over to the federal government and park officials began building the necessary infrastructure. In 1972, the park was opened to the public. The establishment of the park had a tremendous impact on the local communities that surrounded or were adjacent to it.

The relationship between park staff and local residents deteriorated rapidly by the time a decision was made in 1978 to develop a comprehensive management plan to direct future development in the park over the next ten to fifteen years. Although the public was originally supposed to extensively participate in the development of the management plan, the decision was ultimately made without local involvement.

A short time after the management planning exercise was announced, things turned ugly. A park warden was shot at, a bullet was found with a warden's name on it in one of the local lounges park staff were known to frequent, demonstrations against the park were held, lives were threatened, park equipment and facilities were vandalized and secret plans were made to burn the park.

Public Participation

It was at this time Parks Canada officials decided if the park were to survive and be developed for the good of the Canadian people, they would need the support and involvement of the local communities. They decided to hire a consultant and I was contracted by Parks Canada to work as a Public Involvement Facilitator, to involve the public in the preparation of a management plan, which would guide the future development within Gros Morne National Park. My mandate also included training park staff to effectively involve local residents in the decision-making process relative to the operation and maintenance of the park.

Outstanding Park Issues

When I entered the park for the first time in the fall of 1978, there were a number of issues that concerned local residents. These included their right to:

- Harvest wood for domestic fuel purposes
- Harvest wood for commercial purposes
- Snare rabbits to supplement the local food supply
- Hunt moose, bear, lynx, muskrat, beaver and caribou for domestic consumption and the sale of furs
- Free-range domestic cattle and wild horses
- Grazing pasture for cattle and sheep
- Grow vegetables.

Additional issues included:

- The future status of Sally's Cove. Sally's Cove was the only remaining park community. Over half of the community had already left the settlement and the community was designated to be phased out
- The route, design and scheduling of provincial, park and local roads
- The compensation package offered to those who had been expropriated
- The creation of local community councils and corresponding responsibilities for community planning,

zoning, bylaws, the assessment of local properties and buildings and the collection of local taxes—all of which were foreign concepts as far as local residents were concerned prior to the creation of the park

- The picking of bake apples (a local delicacy) and various berries for home use
- The use of park timber by local commercial boat builders
- Permission for local fishermen to carry on their commercial fishing activities while continuing to have access to certain areas now within the jurisdiction of Parks Canada
- The use of park facilities and programs by local residents
- The fact that, except for foreman and laboring jobs, all mid- and senior-management (career) positions with the park were filled by individuals who were not only from outside the local area but were, in many cases, from outside the province
- The attitude of park staff toward local residents. Park staff were discouraged from dating or becoming too friendly with the "locals"
- People feeling "hemmed in" or "surrounded" by the park.

When I entered into discussions with park officials, they insisted on a number of "givens" which were not open to negotiation with the public. These included the future status of Sally's Cove; the harvesting of park resources by local people; the design, location or scheduling of park or provincial roads or highways and the provision of municipal services to the ten remaining local communities.

Before entering the park, I negotiated a change in these givens. I had the concurrence of senior park officials that all issues could be open for dialogue with local and regional groups, as well as with the general Canadian public, as long as I did not create the expectation or promise that issues would be resolved by "giving in" to local demands.

Prior to my arrival at Gros Morne Park headquarters, communications from Parks Canada to the local public had been in written form and included the use of press releases, public notices on bulletin boards and form letters addressed to "Dear householder" or "Dear local resident." These notices invariably informed local residents about park regulations or further restrictions of local activity in or near the park. With the exception of one large "hostile" public meeting held prior to the decision to establish the park, there had been no public or formal discussion on any of the outstanding issues.

The Process

The first step in the process was to convince senior Parks Canada personnel of the value of involving the public in their decision-making process. To accomplish this, a one-week intensive residential workshop was held with senior officials in the department on the subject of public participation. The session included the regional director, all assistant directors, supervisors, heads of sections and park superintendents. It was followed by a similar training session for all middle-management personnel throughout the Atlantic region. I conducted these workshops with the assistance of two public participation consultants.

There were three elements that gave me the opportunity to earn credibility with the local communities, two of which were either beyond my control or due to sheer luck. One was the timing of my entrance. I discovered within hours of talking with local park staff (mostly laborers) that people had reached their boiling point and were getting ready to burn the park within a couple of weeks. I asked them to talk with their friends, relatives and those they considered leaders in their communities about giving me a chance to establish a process for local people to talk with park staff in a meaningful way. The second element that proved to be critical was simply my ability to listen to their feelings as well as their complaints and to ask perceptive questions based on what they told me. I quickly gained a reputation for being a good listener, which went a long way toward building local credibility. The third factor was in no small measure due to the fact that within three hours of entering the region, a local family who was well respected in the region immediately adopted me.

I never tried to explain to anyone that I was a consultant to Parks Canada and not an employee of the park. This was a subtlety unimportant to the "locals." As far as they were concerned, Parks Canada was paying me and I was working for the park.

Upon entering the park area I discovered, with the exception of the hostile activity mentioned earlier, there had been little feedback to staff concerning how local residents felt about the park. Nevertheless, the residents had strong opinions and were outspoken on the subject. In most instances, when I introduced myself as a park representative who was interested in learning how the establishment of a national park had impacted them, it was often the only word I got in for hours. People would respond by stating: "Don't talk to me about the park—I have nothing to say about the park." Then they would continue for hours listing complaints and grievances.

I began my quest by asking two questions: Which community was most upset with the park and who in that community hated the park the most? By six o'clock the first evening, I was in the shed of this person (where he was repairing his lobster traps), listening to his tales of woe concerning how the park had impacted his life. At ten o'clock that night, I was sitting at his kitchen table eating bake apples, while he marveled to his wife that someone representing Parks Canada was actually in his house having a snack with his family. He took great delight in telling me the bake apples we were eating were picked illegally in the park. My host family, who were from the neighboring community, phoned neighbors of this gentleman every hour to see if I was still next door and finally asked them to try and find out how I was making out without letting on why they were there.

Next on my list of priorities was to talk to a commercial boat builder who also disliked the park; he felt the park was threatening his livelihood. Again, a similar experience ensued—by midnight we had moved from his boat building facility to his home for a snack. These experiences were repeated dozens of times in the ten adjacent communities around the park in the following months.

On a more formal basis, I designed a combination of kitchen meetings, open houses and radio programs to provide an opportunity for local residents and park users to talk with park staff. At the first round of these *cuffers* (a local term for the informal small-group discussions which usually took place in a public place, like over the back fence or on the wharf) or open houses, held in eighteen communities, we recorded one hundred and twenty-seven pages of comments in small print on flip-chart sheets. The *cuffers* or open houses were two-day events which began at 10:00 A.M. and lasted until 10:00 P.M. Everything Parks Canada knew about the park was on display in an informal fashion at the events. One of the most popular exhibits included old photos of people and scenery from the area, most of which were supplied by locals. The teams conducting the sessions were on their feet twelve hours a day, six days a week, for six weeks. This did not include setup and dismantling time or travel time to the next community. I would never recommend such an intensive schedule again, although I thought it was necessary at the time.

The *cuffers* gave citizens the opportunity to show their knowledge of the park's resources by recording on maps what they knew about the plants, animals and rocks of the area. They were held in the ten communities surrounded by or adjacent to the park, as well as in eight communities in other parts of Newfoundland, to give other citizens a chance to participate. I worked with park staff before the open houses and during the sessions on how to listen, to ask probing questions and to only record the words of the people—not an interpretation of what was being said.

Before the second round of discussions took place six months later, park officials dealt with each of the comments listed on the flip charts in detail and the results were reported to the community in the form of a newsletter.

Separate but similar processes were used to handle the more difficult issues concerning the future status of Sally's Cove, the routing and scheduling of highways and the development of community development plans.

The Resolution of Park Issues Subsequent to the Public Participation Process

A large number of issues were resolved during the public participation process, including the following:

Issue: Harvesting of wood for domestic purposes.

Resolution: Harvesting of wood for domestic fuel purposes would be permitted in designated areas to a maximum of six cords per household, per season, with a conditional permit governing the methods of cutting and cleanup of the area.

Issue: Harvesting of wood for commercial purposes.

Resolution: The practice would be permitted provided amounts to be cut were determined as a result of a forestry management plan developed by the local association of loggers and based on the principle of regeneration of the resource. Methods were to be acceptable to Parks Canada and permitted in designated areas during designated times.

Issue: The snaring of rabbits to supplement local food supply.

Resolution: The practice was reinstated but restricted to local longtime residents after Canadian Wildlife Service officials advised it would have no appreciable effect on the rabbit population of the park.

Issue: The hunting of park animals for domestic consumption and the sale of furs.

Resolution: Parks Canada was able to convince local residents that hunting was not consistent with the national park philosophy or objectives and could not be permitted in the park.

	Some compensation was paid to those who could prove a loss of income.
Issue:	The grazing of domestic animals and wild horses throughout the park and the use of parkland for growing vegetables.
Resolution:	Parks Canada provided people with assistance in containing their local animals in fenced areas. Adjustments were made to the park boundary to allow longtime local residents to have sufficient land for gardens and domestic animals.
Issue:	The future status of Sally's Cove.
Resolution:	The status of Sally's Cove was changed. A new policy allowed the community to continue to exist, grow and develop in the future. The community's boundary was extended several miles.
Issue:	The route, design and scheduling of provincial, park and local roads.
Resolution:	Parks Canada and the province agreed to involve local people in the design, routing and scheduling of local roads, provincial highways and park roads. I designed a special public participation process to ensure this happened. The first road affected was the one through Sally's Cove. The resulting redesign, prompted by local input, resulted in a two-million-dollar savings when a planned two-mile bypass around the com-

	munity was scrapped in favor of a road through the community.
Issue:	The compensation package offered to those who had been expropriated.
Resolution:	A provincial court of inquiry was held to investigate all complaints and an appeals board with local representation was set up to handle all outstanding grievances.
Issue:	Local municipal concerns and complaints.
Resolution:	The provincial government hired a community planner to provide more training and support to local councils in their planning and administration efforts.
Issue:	Picking bake apples and berries for home use.
Resolution:	Although still officially against park policy, park officials turned a blind eye to the practice as long as it was not abused.
Issue:	The use of park timber for commercial boat builders.
Resolution:	The two local commercial boat builders were permitted to continue the tradition in areas approved by park wardens.
Issue:	Access by commercial fishermen to traditional fishing areas.
Resolution:	Parks Canada agreed to allow the practice to continue without restriction and in most instances assisted the fishermen in making improvements to their landing facilities and storage sheds.

Case Study # 2 — Management Planning in a Tense Environment— Newfoundland and Labrador, Canada

Issue:	The use of park facilities and programs by local people.
Resolution:	Park officials agreed to make more of an effort to have local people use park facilities and in the future agreed to check with residents before designing or building facilities. They would use local residents, especially senior citizens and young people, as park interpreters to tell stories about the local way of life, history and culture to visitors..
Issue:	The hiring of local people for supervisory and career positions.
Resolution:	Parks staff agreed to work more closely with Canadian employment officials, local school boards and the university in preparing people for career positions in the park.
Issue:	The negative attitude of many park staff toward *locals*.
Resolution:	Parks Canada staff was encouraged to take more interest in local affairs and to get involved in the local community.
Issue:	People feeling hemmed in by the park.
Resolution:	The boundaries of the park were adjusted, in one case by several miles, to allow some *breathing space* between the community and the park boundary.

By the end of the three-year management planning process, all outstanding issues had been resolved to the satisfaction of Parks Canada, the local people and the general Canadian public. In order for this to happen it required:

- Changes in federal legislation and national park policies
- Tremendous cooperation and flexibility by all three levels of government
- Awareness of and sensitivity to the need for special consideration regarding local traditions and culture
- The realization by all key participants of the need to trust each other.

The process to accomplish these objectives was the responsibility of the regional director of public participation, working out of the regional office in Halifax.

The first step in the process was getting the regional staff on board. This meant getting them to understand that making provisions for local residents in the Gros Morne area would not undermine national park values and dealing with their dual and sometimes seemingly contradictory mandates of protection and preservation of the natural environments for present and future generations.

It also meant resolving issues in a way that would not open the floodgates across the country for every conceivable use local residents or the general public might want for national parks. By working through various committees and task forces, set up to deal with the issues, the regional coordinator for public participation brought the staff to a consensus on how the issues raised in Gros Morne could be resolved while developing a long-range management plan that respected the values national parks were created to preserve.

The process to achieve this consensus involved establishing clear objectives for each resource the park wanted to protect, appreciating why and how local people wanted to use these resources and attempting to find a common ground based on respect for opposing points of view. In many cases, they were able to reach a compromise. For example, having received sound advice from regional wildlife experts in the Federal Department of Natural Resources, it was determined the snaring of rabbits could be allowed without significantly affecting the long-term rabbit population in the park

However, in another case, it was not possible to find a compromise because of mutually exclusive objectives. Due to safety considerations for park visitors and the overall health of the caribou and moose populations, the department determined that no exception to the exclusion of hunting these animals could be permitted, even in the Gros Morne situation. Once local residents appreciated the Parks Canada dual mandate for preservation and enjoyment of national park resources and experienced the willingness of park officials to consider the input of local residents in decisions directly affecting them, there was a willingness to accept a compromise. In this case, local residents accepted the fact they could no longer hunt moose or caribou in the national park.

Once consensus was achieved at the regional office, a similar process was initiated for personnel at headquarters in Ottawa. In addition to demonstrating that changes in policies were necessary to accommodate the situation at Gros Morne Park, there was the added difficulty of changing federal legislation to reverse the status of Sally Cove from a park community. Nevertheless, as distasteful as this was, there was the realization that if Gros Morne Park was to survive, flexibility on both sides was going to be required—including changing national policy and instituting changes to federal legislation.

We worked with the province of Newfoundland and Labrador and the local authority to oversee the Gros Morne Park Agreement—it was also necessary to work with the Gros Morne Provincial Authority. Once their cooperation and trust was obtained, there were the difficult and complex issues of community planning, natural resource harvesting (wood, fish, and wildlife) and the settlement of compensation for property or lands that were part of the park agreement. The harvesting of wood was particularly difficult. People relied on the resource for house building, firewood and many of their fishing requirements. On the other hand, provincial forestry officials had to maintain a sustainable industry, balancing the needs of local communities with those of the forestry industry. Once the concept of an annual allowable cut, based on good forestry practices of sustainability, was established and accepted, most of the local residents got on board and supported the agreed-upon practices.

The willingness of all parties to work toward difficult and innovative solutions to complex issues was in no small way responsible for Parks Canada and the people of the Gros Morne area of Newfoundland and Labrador to live in harmony. This was not accomplished overnight but took several years to achieve.

Although new issues often arise, there is a well entrenched process for handling and resolving problems. The people in the Gros Morne National Park area now have a harmonious relationship with the park and park visitors as well as their local environment.

Chapter 9

Study # 3 — Community Planning from the Inside Out —Marathon, Ontario, Canada

A Brief History

Marathon, as this community is now known, was once called Peninsula Harbour. It is evident that some form of human civilization existed in these parts of North Superior possibly as long ago as 155 B.C. The early inhabitants had no written language and therefore left no recorded history. Indian inhabitants, mainly of the Ojibway nation, occupied sand beaches at the mouth of the Pic River and surrounding areas as long ago as 500 B.C. It is probable Gabriel Cote, who built the first trading post between 1790 and 1792, established the earliest white settlement at the mouth of the Pic.

The town of Marathon is located on the north shore of Lake Superior, approximately 300 kilometers east of Thunder Bay and 400 kilometers west of Sault Ste. Marie, along Trans-Canada Highway #17.

The written history of Marathon dates back to 1885 when Peninsula Harbour (now Marathon) played a significant role in the construction of the Canadian Pacific Railway through the north shore route of Lake Superior, which one engineer described as "two hundred miles of engineering impossibility." The peninsula was one of the most difficult and costly phases of the entire construction program. An estimated 12,000 men worked out of Peninsula Harbour on the railroad, utilizing up to 5,000 horses.

A turning point in the history of Peninsula Harbour occurred in 1944 when Marathon Paper Mills of Canada constructed a mill and the area was renamed.

Marathon continued as a mill town for almost 40 years until the discovery of one of the world's richest gold deposits in Hemlo, 40 kilometers east of Marathon, in the early 1980s. Projections indicated the mines had a life of 30 years. Over the last several years Marathon's population has grown from 2,500 to almost 6,000.

Although there was a great deal of exploration in the surrounding area, the mining situation stabilized in the late '80s. A proposed $335 million expansion of a Kraft pulp mill operation was put on hold until the global outlook for the sale of pulp improved. Even so, the James River Corporation, an international paper company, committed itself to a boiler expansion program in the summer of 1992 worth $16 million.

Even though the town had weathered a recent recession better than most communities in Canada, the town was anxious to diversify local economic activity in preparation for a new global economy that was already emerging. The creation of an Economic Development Commission (March 1992) and the preparation of an economic development strategy were the first steps in the process of taking responsibility for and control of their future.

The study area was defined as the town of Marathon and the surrounding area from which resources could be drawn in order to create economic diversification.

The Approach

There were five key variables critical to implementing an effective community development strategy. They were put in order of importance: people, people, people, people and people. An effective strategic process and a clear statement of its objectives were important, as were concrete criteria and the development of appropriate measurement procedures for judging success. The key challenge was identifying the people who would not only have a *stake* in the impact of an economic strategy but who also felt a strong enough need for such an initiative that they would willingly participate in the process of developing one. *Ownership* was critical.

Although the first step had to ensure community consensus that a need for a development strategy existed, it was equally important to recognize that all stakeholders (or interest groups) were a piece of the puzzle and that all had perspectives—and information—that needed to be taken into account. It was tempting to rely heavily on individuals who already held positions of power or status in the community but doing so posed two problems. First, they would not necessarily be the people who would devote the highest degree of enthusiasm and commitment to the process. Research had shown that more could be accomplished by working with someone at a lower level in the power structure, even if the individual was in a position of authority in the community. Second, it might overlook individuals or groups who exerted informal moral or social support influence in the community (such as community volunteer workers) or who came from a sector of the community that was often voiceless but would still be affected by policy decisions.

These, then, were the guidelines followed in initiating Marathon's community development strategy. It is important to note that what fundamentally distinguished the approach from others was this: the burden of making choices about the nature, purpose, content and methods of proceeding did not rest with one person or one agency. The decisions were shared by identifiable and organized groups of intended users. They were organized in the sense that they were brought together, face-to-face, as a group or task force to work on and participate in making decisions about the process and the end result. It meant that in the initial phase the focus was on identifying individuals in the community who were enthusiastic, familiar with the *culture* and who either possessed or had access to information relevant to the particular community's economic, social and cultural development issues and problems.

At this stage there was no attempt to identity or involve specific organizations or levels of government but to ensure those developing the comprehensive plan were familiar with (and sensitive to) the varied and multiple interests in their own community. Experience has shown it is not organizations or agencies per se that effectively develop, interpret and implement policies, but the presence of caring, competent people—most often, frontline people—within organizations, who make the difference. They are the ones who have the most realistic knowledge as to what works and what doesn't in their particular community.

The premise underlying these guidelines was this: any strategy must be developed by those who knew their community, knew what was feasible in their community and who were fully aware of how useful the strategy would be to those who would live with it.

The high quality of participation that occurred in the development of Marathon's community development strategy reflected the application of the guidelines described above. Local citizens also benefited from a series of five workshops on group decision-making and consensus building, goal setting and information-gathering skills. Also important to success was the inclusion of policy makers (*idea people*) and policy implementers (*practical people*) from the beginning of the planning process.

The efforts and risks involved in working interactively with politicians, civil servants and special interest groups were considerable but the potential payoff of having them involved in solving their problems was worth the risk. At stake was improving the effectiveness of government at all three levels in responding to meaningful involvement by a broad cross section of people and hopefully making not only the programs but also the bureaucrats accountable to the people they were supposed to serve. It embodied the highest essence of the democratic process.

Principles

Although specific recommendations should reflect the uniqueness of a community, there were a number of general principles underlying successful community economic development strategies:

- Clearly understood objectives, authorities and protocols were in place

- Ownership of the process was invested in those who would continue to be affected by the outcome
- Required information and data was accurately compiled
- Data was made available in easily understood and usable formats
- The opportunity for the interpretation of such data and information was offered within the community.

The Marathon Phased Approach

Commitment to the community development planning process was exhibited in two ways: 1) Marathon's town council mandated the promotion of community economic development; and 2) the town voted that a portion of its budget go toward economic development.

The following is an outline of the phased approach that was used to develop a dynamic strategy to diversify the economy. The strategy was flexible due to the changing nature of the local economy. But, just as important, the town council was flexible. Six months after being appointed, the Marathon Economic Development Commission returned to council with a request to have its mandate enlarged to include all social and economic aspects of community development and they requested a name change to that effect.

Wonderful things took place in the first six months. The only instruction I gave to the commission was that they operate in a *nontraditional manner*; I did not define what I meant. Because many of the people on the commission were busy and they couldn't find one night of the month when everyone was free to meet, they made their first nontraditional decision, agreeing to meet from 6:30 A.M. to 8:00 A.M. so no one would have to lose work time. The members arrived at 6:00 A.M. for coffee, doughnuts and socializing so meetings began and ended on time. Meetings only went past 8:00 A.M. twice.

It was decided that the chairperson would not be the manager of the local paper mill or the manager of two of the local gold mines. The commission hit another milestone when they decided to make all decisions by *consensus* and not by voting. Nothing would proceed if it did not have the unanimous support of the commission. They experienced differences of opinions as a positive and encouraged each other to voice reservations or objections to anything under discussion. They learned to work through and value conflict, not avoid it.

Phase One

The Marathon Community Development Commission, appointed by town council and the manager of economic development agreed to take on the following tasks:

1.) The preparation of an historical and cultural perspective related to the development of the town of Marathon.

2.) The development of a community database, updated to include:

- Demographics
- Land Use
- Infrastructure
- Municipal Services
- Municipal Debt
- Sources of Investment Capital.

3.) A review of current economic development efforts, made by organizations and agencies operating within the town of Marathon.

4.) The creation of a sector-specific *economic health* analysis for:

- Mining/Minerals
- Tourism
- Forestry
- Education, Postsecondary Education
- Government Services
- Service Industry
- Transportation
- Lake Superior Development
- High-tech (Fiber Optics—Global Trends Info Highway)

*Phase Two**

*The model used to guide efforts at this junction was adapted from a development card for the United States entitled *Making The Grade* published by the Corporation of Enterprise Development in Washington, D. C.

Taking measure of a *local economy* was not a simple task. Every provincial economy was different and even within provinces there were major differences, such as the economies of northern versus southern Ontario. In fact, the growth requirement of each business sector was unique.

A critical question they asked was: How would they recognize an economy with a supportive environment for business development under today's competitive conditions? What were the indicators of whether it was a good place for business to grow?

The commission asked four questions to determine how healthy a local economy was:

- How well was the economy providing the opportunity for a better quality of life.
- How healthy were the businesses comprising the local economy?
- What was the capacity for expanding growth and opportunity?

- What policies had the local council established to help foster business growth and economic opportunity?

#1—Performance Index

No business was interested in expanding or locating to an area that was dying economically. It was important to remember that business development was not an end in itself. The bottom line was whether Marathon was a good place for businesses to grow and whether the town was providing opportunities for a richer and better life. It was amazing how the traditional definitions of business climate were completely ignored using this most basic measure of economic strength and attractiveness. Job quality, equity and quality of life issues were not regarded as important economic indicators in traditional approaches to industrial development. The Marathon Community Development Commission needed to recognize these three factors, plus employment (growth, unemployment rate, duration rate and status of displaced workers), as well as income (earned income per capita, income change per capita, percent below the poverty line), in order to know how the town would measure up.

#2—Vitality Index

Survival of Marathon's economy would depend on fostering the expansion of young, small businesses, spawning new firms and ensuring innovation in the large industrial companies. In order to evaluate this, two criteria were used:

- Competitiveness (international exports, manufacturing investment per production worker, percent of high growth companies)
- Entrepreneurial energy (business foundation rates, self-employment rates and minority and women business ownership).

#3—Capacity Index

The decision of a business to start up, expand or relocate to Marathon was determined by three factors:

- The availability of labor (appropriately trained workers, technicians and managers)
- The accessibility of financial capital
- The adequacy of infrastructure (roads, water, sewer, and so forth)

#4—Policies Index

The old maxim, "the government which governs best, governs least," was not entirely accurate anymore. Perhaps a better way to say it was "the government that governs best, governs thoughtfully." Increasingly, governments at all levels and private industry were working in partnerships to achieve economic development objectives they were unable to achieve individually.

In order to be on the top of any investor's list, Marathon needed policies and programs that would:

- Improve the three levels of government business regulations and control (making them more responsive to local business needs)
- Create an effective and equitable tax code
- Provide easily accessible capital
- Provide support for technology and business development
- Build and maintain public works
- Invest in human resources.

In other words, Marathon needed a report card on how well it was doing in relation to these four indexes.

Phase Three

Based on the information generated as a result of the completion of phases one and two, an economic development strategy was formulated.

The strategy involved:

A) Recommendations that encouraged economic development in Marathon by identifying the community's strengths and weaknesses and the major blocks to development, be they social or economic.

B) Identifying target sectors and specific opportunities for economic development in Marathon. For example:

- Providing value added opportunities in the resource sectors (forestry, mining, fishing, tourism and so on)
- Attracting industries or businesses to a new industrial park
- Finding commercial establishments that would prosper in Marathon
- Putting in place prosperity support elements that were lacking
- Optimizing the size and population.

C) Defining an implementation structure for the Marathon economic development strategy. For example:

- Community Development Commission/Marathon and District Chamber of Commerce
- Cooperative Roles and Responsibilities
- Economic Development Manager
- Roles and Responsibilities
- Business Development Venture Capital Center
- Roles and Organization Structure
- Options
- Postsecondary Education and Regional Training Structures

D) Utilizing the information generated from the above objectives in order to prepare a sound economic development strategy for the town of Marathon.

E) Making recommendations for an implementation plan on the basis of good economic principles and not based on a perception of what may or may not be acceptable, including:

- Emerging global trends
- An assessment of national and provincial priorities and strategies or lack thereof
- Marathon's *niche* in a larger context
- Identification of priorities
- Various bottom line and ideal options to achieve each objective with a preferred option indicated
- Costs and financial implications for each option recommended
- A flow chart indicating a schedule of activities and time frames
- An executive summary of the comprehensive strategy

What's happened since the strategy was developed?

With the comprehensive community development plan in place, Marathon turned its attention to the need for a regional development strategy for the Lake Superior area of northern Ontario. The first step in the initiative was to get the two large cities of Sault Ste. Marie and Thunder Bay to see themselves as gateways to the north Superior Region and not simply as destination locations. Early efforts at co-operating on mutual objectives involved creating discount golf and ski packages so members from local clubs could travel to the regional shopping centers at special discount prices and vice versa. This was simply an acknowledgement that many people from smaller communities traveled to larger cities on a regular basis. The new discount packages encouraged people from the larger cities to travel to smaller communities for a sporting experience combined with other unique cultural activities and small town experiences. Following the success of these initiatives, the communities agreed to cooperate on a mutual marketing plan selling the *region* of northern Lake Superior to visitors and not just each community. The results were a win-win situation.

In the last few years attention has turned to working with the communities within a two-hundred-kilometer radius to cooperate and complement each other's local strategies and take full advantage of the limited resources each community has available for economic development. It also meant a commitment not to compete with each other in trying to attract businesses to their region.

The prevailing attitude acknowledged that real competition comes from farther away and they could gain more by having a united front than by competing with each other. The communities agreed to focus on what was in the best interest of the region, making individual goals secondary to what was good for the whole. There was faith that the approach put the interest of clients first and with such a strategy, each community would eventually receive its share of the benefits.

Chapter 10

Case Study # 4 — Rising from Hopelessness into a NewERA — New Waterford, Cape Breton Island, Nova Scotia, Canada

Background

The New Waterford and District communities are situated on the east side of Cape Breton Island, in the northern corner of the Cape Breton Regional Municipality (CBRM) along the coast of the Atlantic Ocean.

The town of New Waterford is 5.6 kilometers long and is surrounded by the communities of Lingan, River Ryan, Scotchtown, New Victoria and Victoria Mines. The New Waterford area is 18 kilometers from Sydney and about 12 kilometers from the Sydney Airport. There are several road routes to New Waterford and the district from Sydney and Glace Bay. Incorporated as a municipality in 1913, New Waterford's population is approximately 7,200 (1997) with another 4,000 persons in the surrounding communities. The area has been historically centered on the coal mining industry. The men of the New Waterford area have been mining coal for over 100 years. The last coal mine within the original town boundary closed in 1973. In 1988, the town successfully annexed the land (later to become part of CBRM) on which two collieries (Lingan and Phalen) stood. With the Cape Breton Development Corporation's (DEVCO) announcement in 1999 that it was closing the Phalen Mine, coal mining in the New Waterford area ceased. Since the most recent downsizing in 1996, at least 450 to 600 individuals or approximately 37 percent of the DEVCO workforce have been negatively impacted along with the communities in which they reside.

The negative economic impact was not new to New Waterford and District. The decline in the demand for coal in the early 1950s resulted in the systematic closure of some coal mines throughout Cape Breton Island. The New Waterford area, like other mining towns, fell victim to the consequences of economic and population decline. Businesses suffered, families moved from the communities and the area struggled to survive. However, with the opening of two new mines (Lingan and Phalen) in the 1970s and 1980s, a new vitality returned to the area for over a decade.

Case Study # 4 — Rising from Hopelessness into a New-ERA — New Waterford, Cape Breton Island, Nova Scotia, Canada

A number of communities on Cape Breton Island have established formal economic and community development organizations to diversity their economies over the years; however, the New Waterford area did not establish a formal community development organization until NewERA was established.

Context

The four individuals who originally formed the New Waterford and District Economic Renewal Association (NewERA) came together in the spring of 1998. They later expanded the group and reached out to surrounding communities to see what could be done to revitalize New Waterford and District (Lingan, River Ryan, Scotchtown, New Waterford, New Victoria and Victoria Mines). The group has worked together with the hope of involving all six communities in a process to develop a comprehensive community development plan that would lead to the renewal of the area.

With this purpose in mind, the group became incorporated in October 1999 and created a vision statement (their identity, their values) for the District for the year 2020: "Through a renewed community spirit and our own creativity, the people of this area have restored our economic well-being while retaining our sense of history and tradition." Their mission statement (what they needed to do to achieve their vision) was: "To aid the community to develop a sound structure which will strive to meet the socio-economic needs of the people and to foster a healthy quality of life."

NewERA also established its main objectives:

- Obtain full participation in the planning process from a cross section of residents in the geographic area
- Acquire and obtain the knowledge, understanding, and skills necessary to develop a comprehensive community development plan for a revitalized community
- Have the community legitimize the association.

The initial group hoped the development of a comprehensive (all-inclusive—social, economic, health, environment, recreation, culture, history, values) community development plan would take place in the context of NewERA's vision, mission and objectives. Through a series of workshops and a day-and-a-half seminar, NewERA defined community development as, "a process through which local citizens of all ages plan and work together to improve the quality of life in their community, thereby restoring community control, pride, self-esteem and hope for the future."

One of the first tasks NewERA accomplished was developing a community profile. A research project funded by Human Resources Development Canada (HRDC) and NewERA prepared a document containing:

- Statistical data and historical information on the people and the six communities
- The identification and location of natural resources, especially those that are unique to the area and the general condition of the local environment to sustain certain kinds of development
- The physical infrastructure (a listing of water and sewer services, public buildings, commercial space, roads, mass media and modern communications)
- A list of the groups and organizations in the region.

NewERA used various methods to gather ideas from the community. It approached seventy-six organizations and groups and met with those that accepted an invitation to talk about how they could jointly plan for the future of the district. Questionnaires were distributed at class reunions and a full-page ad in the local press invited residents to submit their ideas on how they would like to see their area developed. NewERA's coordinator met with students in the local regional high school. Academics and economists from outside the New Waterford area were also asked what ideas or thoughts they had in regard to how New Waterford and district might develop.

Because of the limited funding available, NewERA was not able to enter into a comprehensive community development planning exercise as originally envisaged. Instead, NewERA had to settle for the development of a strategic action plan focusing on what conditions they needed to create for a healthy local economy. This was narrower in scope than the original concept but more manageable given their limited funds.

In the fall of 2000, working with an associate of mine, Blaine Gillis, I helped NewERA hold a series of six open houses to involve residents who were interested in preparing a strategic plan for their communities. The first three open houses, held in community halls around the District, provided the people with the opportunity to visit with NewERA board of directors, staff and consultants over an extended period.

In excess of five thousand newsletters were delivered to households in the six communities. In an invitation from the chairperson, Ronald J. MacDonald, Ron reminded them that, "although the history of this area has been that we have allowed others to plan our future, we, the residents, now have the opportunity to do it for ourselves. The people of New Waterford and District, with knowledge and understanding of our economy, can take ownership of our own plan. When we do this, and only then, will there be real change in the way decisions are made that affect us. So, beginning today, let's plan our future together."

The first four pages of the newsletter contained imaginary articles of success stories that could appear in the local newspaper in the year 2020. They were intended to inspire people to imagine what their communities could be like if they were able to achieve their wildest dreams. The remainder of the publication dealt with what they would have to do to close the gap between what is now and what they want to be in the future. It also gave details on the open houses and how residents could participate in planning their own future.

People were encouraged to drop in between 11:00 A.M. and 8:00 P.M. and stay as long as they liked. They were given the opportunity to comment on, add to or correct the research data NewERA had gathered dealing with:

- A comprehensive community profile of the district
- The natural resources and environment of the area
- Ownership and zoning
- An up-to-date aerial map of the area where people could write their comments directly on a map

The atmosphere was relaxed and informal with light refreshments provided. The intent was to create an environment that was familiar to people in the area, namely, *kitchen meetings*. The technique was part of the People's School movement, modeled after the work of extension workers from St. Francis Xavier University in the forties and fifties. The essence of each person's input was recorded on flip charts and people were asked to check the accuracy of the recordings before they left the hall.

Five weeks after the first set of open houses, a second set of open houses was held to review a draft of the strategic directions, goals and action steps developed as a result of the first open houses. It was also an opportunity to review the analysis done by the NewERA board of directors and the consultants and for residents to provide further input on the final plan.

A week prior to the second set of open houses, a second newsletter was distributed to households reporting the results of their participation to date. The opinions of people who attended the open houses were reported in detail and the four themes of strategic directions were listed:

- Enhancement of New Waterford and District
- Refocus Community (Downtown) Core
- Enterprise Growth
- Infrastructure Improvements for Enterprise.

Each strategic direction had a strategic objective stating what needed to be accomplished, followed by a series of specific goals or initiatives relating to that objective. This was followed by a set of strategies or action steps needed to carry the idea or project forward.

Space was provided in the newsletter for residents to write down comments to bring to the second set of open houses.

Over seven hundred people were consulted or actively participated in the development of the strategic plan. NewERA was now in the process of changing its role into one of facilitating and overseeing the implementation of the plan. NewERA's board of directors' progress to date was contained in an executive summary of their latest workshop.

EXECUTIVE SUMMARY

At 1:00 P.M., Monday, January 29, 2001, eight members of the NewERA board of directors and the coordinator met at Carmel Center, New Waterford, with two facilitators to:

- Identify the role of NewERA in relation to the Strategic Community Action Plan
- Prepare a *plan of action* to implement the strategic plan
- Develop an organizational structure that would enable the board to fulfill its role.

By 3:15 P.M. they had the following tasks outlined and had identified their success to date. Evaluation of NewERA indicated:

> Satisfactory performance to date, culminating in a strategic community action

> A plan in which a cross section of the community was involved in the planning process

> Acquisition of knowledge, understanding and skills of the planning process

> Community sanction to spearhead implementation of the plan

> Confirmation of vision and mission statements

> Agreement on validity of NewERA's general

objectives
> Criteria for deciding priorities in strategic plan
> List of priorities identified
> The relationship of priorities for plan implementation to directions, strategic objectives and specific goals
> Specific goals and guidelines of projects for the revised proposal for funding
> A two-month period to clarify NewERA's role and restructure if necessary
> A task force to recommend applicable amendments to the constitution and bylaws.

In conclusion, the participants found the workshop worthwhile and had provided them with the tools to pursue a funding proposal as the next step to, "continue its role with increased technical and professional functions in order to oversee and facilitate the implementation of the strategic plan."

As of February 2002, NewERA's new board of directors, consisting of fourteen people, had several contracts in place with the Human Resources Development Canada (HRDC) and Enterprise Cape Breton Corporation (ECBC) totaling more than $550,000 for the following projects, which were identified in the NewERA community strategic plan:

- Sponsor an entrepreneurship development program which involved contracting the YMCA Enterprise

Center to deliver guidance to prospective entrepreneurs in the New Waterford area

- Sponsor a youth internship program designed to provide youth between the ages of eighteen and thirty with advice on how to become more employable, as well as arranging work placements
- Maintain NewERA office and staff, necessary to coordinate community development activities
- Sponsor a consultant's study on the feasibility of turning the former Lingan/Phalen mine site into an industrial business park
- Sponsor a feasibility study into the construction of a business incubator/office building in downtown New Waterford
- Sponsor a study into a downtown improvement initiative; put together a plan to improve the appearance and structure of the downtown shopping district
- Sponsor the production of twenty-six murals to depict the history of the New Waterford area, to be placed at various locations throughout the community
- Sponsor a study by the New Waterford Wellness Center Committee into the development of a wellness complex adjacent to the Breton Education Center, which would include an artificial turf soccer field, a fitness center, an expanded tennis facility and a new hardwood floor in the BEC's smaller gym.

Chapter 11

Where Do We Go from Here?

I started this book with the question, “If jobs are not the answer, then what is?” It only seems appropriate therefore that it should end with a question. However, getting the question right is half the battle to coming up with a successful answer. The questions we need to ask are: What does the future of work hold for us? How can we respond to the crisis of the lack of permanent, meaningful, well-paying, sustainable jobs? Joblessness and job insecurity afflict many sectors of society globally. As mentioned in the introduction, jobs are being lost, downsized, shifted overseas and automated out of existence.

Yet, we are confronted with an even deeper crisis—a personal, spiritual void of meaning and celebration in our work. Why is work so burdensome to many? Many people find their work unfulfilling, stressful or boring. Add to this the increasing insecurity of job positions and the threat of layoffs, together with the loss of trust among employees when companies downsize, despite higher company profits and increased worker productivity. The explanation for this is complex but some elements include the industrial model of work, with workers fixed in rigid assembly-line systems; the hierarchical structures of management over labor; the consumerism cycles of working to spend; and the fact that so much work in the industrial age is destructive, destroying both the environment and workers' spirits.

We need a different model of work from the traditional industrial model if we are to get out of the crisis successfully. As always, however, this crisis also presents us with opportunities—to rethink work and to rebuild the values that strengthen the meaning of work in our daily lives and in our society. The very word crisis can leave people feeling paralyzed and disempowered. As mentioned, more helpful is the Chinese symbol for crisis, which includes elements of the symbols for both danger and opportunity. This response has two dimensions. On a spiritual level, rituals that release the stresses of work, celebrate our vocation or calling and connect human work to divine creativity can help us find a deeper perspective on the purpose of our work and our leisure time.

On a workplace level, many grassroots initiatives are already emerging to overcome the industrial model of work. These include worker-ownership of businesses and the spread of worker self-management and teamwork. Several times a year I work for the National Training Laboratories Institute in Virginia providing professional training experiences for Fortune 500 companies' senior executives. Most of the companies are now using new strategies to involve their workers in a meaningful way through such techniques as: self-managed work teams; workplace democracy, which links the success of the individual with the success of the organization; the process of lifelong learning, with employees rewarded for developing their skills and innovations; and shorter workweeks. As citizens, we can empower ourselves to move beyond our immediate work crisis to a new paradigm for understanding work and our roles in the economy. These responses describe steps we can take to promote meaningful, dignified work in sustainable communities.

We can also challenge ourselves on how to think differently about the challenges around the concept of work—in other words, to *think outside the box*. If we do, we can begin to imagine the possibility of creating our own future rather than just reacting to the trends of the marketplace. This allows us to think in terms of empowering ourselves rather than waiting to be empowered by someone or something.

In the past, we tended to see economic power as power over others and therefore possessed predominantly by global corporations and financial markets with their control over labor and the earth's resources. Another kind of power challenges the dominance of economic markets—the *rela-*

tional power that flows from citizen action as people use information, knowledge, teamwork and shared decision making to create change. That power reminds us economies were created to serve people—not the other way around—and we can take back control of our resources and livelihoods.

There are other ways we can empower ourselves. We can reclaim economic power as consumers and investors. Every market decision we make—where to buy clothes, what kind of food to eat, where to bank, how to invest retirement savings—makes someone else richer and rewards them for their market behavior. Consumers wield an enormous power to *vote with their pocketbooks* and have achieved some remarkable victories. The consumer campaign against Nestlé led to the development of international standards for infant formula, saving the lives of tens of thousands of children around the globe.

More and more people are beginning to realize they are also major players in the giant financial markets that create and eliminate jobs. Through pension plans and mutual fund investments, many average workers own a piece of multinational corporations and other huge publicly-traded businesses. With this realization of power comes a strong demand for *socially responsible* businesses—businesses that demonstrate responsibility toward workers, the environment and communities.

If we think about our power as voters, then we can realize we have the power to influence economic policy through our elected representatives and we can become shapers of economic policies by joining with others to make job issues a national priority. As workers and employers, we can bring more democratic values into the process of finding and keeping a job.

There is one thing we can be certain of these days: jobs are scarce. The official unemployment rate in Atlantic Canada ranges from 10 to 20 percent, depending on where you look or whose figures you believe. There are hundreds of thousands of people out of work in our country at any given time. For the most part, these are people who want to work full-time but either don't have jobs or can only find part-time positions. There are also thousands and thousands who work year-round, full-time but still earn less than the poverty level for a family of four. Even in areas of relatively low unemployment, the number of job seekers far exceeds the number of available full-time jobs, especially for job seekers with no post-high-school training or for those in poor areas. On a global level, millions of people are unemployed as rapid technological change and corporate downsizing pushes millions of people out of the workforce.

The reality is, there is no end of work to be done. Our ability to create jobs is limited only by our imagination and our willingness to make work a priority for investment. Unmet social needs in our communities abound. We need teachers for our public schools, preventive health care, affordable housing, environmental cleanup and safer neighborhoods.

Some of the work needed in homes and communities is being done now—free. The social economy produces and distributes goods and services outside the traditional *money economy* most of us enter when we go to work. Women do much of the work in the social economy: caring for homes, children and aging parents. The social economy also produces public services, like neighbors pitching in to clean up an empty lot. The social economy provides an enormously rich source of livelihoods—if we are willing to transfer profits from the money economy to support stronger families, schools, neighborhoods and communities.

How can we make the investment needed to transform work into jobs? One option is to have a national job-creation strategy that, as the private business sector sheds jobs, the public sector—government—would redirect its energies to help develop a community-based volunteer sector. This *third force* could include thousands of nonprofit organizations, which already contribute significantly to the economy. Another policy option, for those permanently unemployed by productivity advances and technological change, is to put these people to work rebuilding neighborhoods and local infrastructure. This could be done through tax deductions for hours of volunteer service (a *shadow wage*) and a social wage (guaranteed income) for community service.

The Canadian public could be asked to support specific tax changes to finance these workers. If we really wanted to do something about *the unemployed*, we could guarantee full employment through a comprehensive program of public-sector job creation. There will be critics who claim public job creation programs are costly. However, it is worth exploring to see if the real savings from full employment, both in terms of money saved from other programs and increased social well-being, would outweigh the costs. These are not entirely new proposals but each of these suggestions—to translate work into jobs—raises questions as well as possibilities, and each deserves full discussion and debate.

Some new initiatives to invest in meaningful livelihoods are already beginning to take hold. For example, many communities are moving outside the traditional money economy to barter and exchange with their own local currency. Often, these local exchange trading systems facilitate a marketplace that invests in work often not valued equally in commercial markets. One such system I had the opportunity to experience a few years ago was the Cape Ann dollars local exchange system in Gloucester, northeast of Boston, Massachusetts. The way it works is simple and legal—Cape Ann dollars (C.A.$) are paper currency local to Cape Ann. Local individuals and businesses use the currency to buy goods and services from each other. Membership is just $5 U.S. and in return for becoming a member you get 40 C.A.$ and a year-long directory listing under the category of your choice. If someone is not interested in being a listed member in the directory but wants to support the local economic activity by putting more C.A.$ into circulation, they can exchange U.S. dollars for Cape Ann dollars at an exchange rate of 1C.A.$ for 1U.S. dollar.

Another example is Ithaca *HOURS* (worth 10U.S. dollars), in Ithaca, New York, which are used to exchange services and goods such as child care, fresh produce, home repair services and even dental care. The currency, which circulates within the community to put people to work, buys everything from roofing to nursing care and bike repair.

Even the U.S. Congress is beginning to explore possibilities that go beyond *free market* principles to invest in community-based work that meets real social needs. The Agriculture Committee of the U.S. House of Representatives recently approved legislation—the Community Food Security Act—to provide up to $2.5 million annually in grants for community-based food security projects, especially those that develop low-income communities and help sustain small farmers.

In the U.S., the Women's Environment and Development Organization has developed community report cards that enable communities to assess their needs in the areas of health, environment and development. U.S. cities have developed their own indicators to evaluate local conditions with respect to health, education, poverty, race relations, environment, energy efficiency and other key measures of social progress. Jacksonville, Florida, has used quality-of-life indicators since 1983.

A movement to build real sustainability in U.S. cities and regions has emerged since the Earth Summit held in Rio in June 1992 produced *Agenda 21*. Cities such as Seattle, New York and Washington, D.C. and the states of Hawaii, Kentucky and Vermont are taking inventory of work they need to do to become *sustainable.* In building a movement that demands environmental and economic justice, they call into question the existing ways of organizing the U.S. economy. Maybe it's time for Canada to do likewise.

We have two excellent examples in the industrial area of Sydney, on Cape Breton Island, of community development organizations that have successfully addressed the issue of development from a business perspective. New Dawn Enterprises was one of the first community business development corporations in Canada. It was founded in 1974 by a group of local people concerned with the economic decline of the region. New Dawn started out providing affordable housing for people on low or medium incomes, job creation projects, a senior citizen home, a community resource center and home nursing and dental centers. It now has over twenty million dollars in assets and has a business structure with sufficient flexibility to respond to a variety of community needs. A more recent example is BCA Holdings, a community finance corporation with over a million dollars in assets. It raises investment money, invests in local job-creating businesses and pays a return on investment to local investors. BCA has come to the aid of a number of near-bankrupt companies, such as a high-tech rope company and a radio station. It is now in the process of building a four- to five-million-dollar high-rise condominium in downtown Sydney.

Neither BCA Holdings nor New Dawn Enterprises have received government grants to date.

There is no doubt the loss of a job can severely hurt an individual worker, causing emotional and physical health problems and stress on his or her family. Plant closings and widespread unemployment can devastate entire communities, as has been experienced on Cape Breton Island where the coal and steel industries have been closed by the federal and provincial governments in the past year or so.

On Cape Breton Island, as well as across the country, communities are working successfully to rebuild their local economies. An important first step in this process, and a sign of hope in today's work crisis, is the movement toward community inventories of social progress, work needing to be done and grassroots initiatives to do the work.

I can't think of a better way to end this book than to quote Silver Donald Cameron from an article in the *Halifax Chronicle Herald* of December 5, 2000: "Active associations and self-reliant communities create citizens, proud and productive people whose gifts are used and valued. In the end, community development is not about enterprises, structures and programs. It is about the development of people. Are we finally beginning to grasp that simple truth?" I certainly hope so.

Epilogue

As mentioned in the preface, it is my hope that many people reading this book will be interested in carrying on a dialogue concerning the issues raised in the preceding chapters. It was not my intention to provide answers about the nature and meaning of work but rather to share the struggle many of the people I had the privilege of working with over the years went through as they tried to answer these questions. It was as much a learning process for me as I hope it was for them. I know I certainly learned more and received more than I taught or gave.

As illustrated in the first two chapters, my desire is always to enter into discussions with people, whenever the occasion arises or can be created, with the intention of stimulating thinking on any particular subject of mutual interest. As my daughter Dawn Michelle put it, "He just helps them with whatever is bothering them." Given proper support and encouragement I think most of us would be happy to spend our lives learning to improve our minds for the sole purpose of leaving this planet in a better condition than we found it. One of the best ways to do this is to learn how to think logically and critically about important questions that concern us. In order to do this well, we must learn to ask useful questions and to constantly improve the difficult task of saying clearly what we mean, in such a way that we can carry on an intelligent dialogue about things of interest or concern to us and those around us. Part of the skill to thinking critically is the ability to think outside the box, not to assume what seems obvious but to constantly identify our basic assumptions and to bring these assumptions into question.

One useful technique I have tried to demonstrate throughout the book, is how to frame a question in such a manner that it causes people to think about the question differently. Often this can be as simple as putting the question in the exact opposite framework than we are used to thinking of it. A couple of examples may serve to illustrate this point.

For years, I have tried to figure out how much money I/we need to live more or less comfortably in our present circumstances. One day I reframed the question and began to think of it in terms of how little I/we need to live. The interesting thing I discovered was, that by reframing the question, I came up with an entirely different answer.

Epilogue

When I went to work for the city of Thompson in northern Manitoba as manager of economic development, one of my first tasks was to participate in a committee on doctor recruitment. The community of sixteen thousand was down to four doctors. At the first meeting I attended, I challenged the committee members to think outside the box and suggested we didn't need to recruit doctors to our community. They thought I was crazy. I suggested we recruit people instead. Then they knew for sure I was crazy. When they understood what I was asking them to do, the entire approach to getting doctors in the north changed and we became much more successful in our efforts. My point was this: Our long-term objective was not simply to get doctors to our community but to keep them there as long as possible. The city of Thompson had a reputation, especially among professionals, for having transient residents who made lots of money and then went elsewhere to enjoy *the good life*. After much debate, the recruitment committee came to the conclusion that if we concentrated our pitch for recruiting *people* rather than doctors, then our approach would be quite different. However, we wanted these people to have medical degrees. If we considered them first as individuals and not as doctors, then we would be sensitive to their needs as *persons*. These people might be single, young, unattached or with a significant other. In some instances, they might be inexperienced (certainly in northern conditions and medicine) or married, maybe not so young, with a family and the fear of leaving an extended family. Being five hundred miles from the major medical facilities in Winnipeg, Manitoba, there was also the question of professional development, specialized equipment and backup expertise that was not available in the north. By reframing the question, the issues of how to make them quickly feel a part of a community, how to give them a positive orientation toward the advantages of living in the north and appreciating an enriched outdoor lifestyle and how to have them appreciate the tremendous advantages of living in a multicultural community, became the focus of our efforts to market *the north* to people unfamiliar with it. Ultimately, Thompson went from four to over a dozen doctors in less than a year, with many of them deciding to stay indefinitely.

It is my hope that by reading this book, you will find your curiosity stimulated to the point where you will begin to ask your own questions and think about the important social and economic questions facing us as a society. No matter what your station in life, you will believe the experts have not done a particularly good job of addressing the serious problems we face. They have done an especially poor job of anticipating the important questions facing us as we enter this century and of helping us prepare to answer these with innovative solutions to some very old problems.

Therefore, I challenge you to think about the concepts and theories presented here and the basis of the evidence provided for what worked and why. Also, I ask you to think about how these examples compare with your own experience, your other readings and other research in the field. Then, I hope you will begin to ask questions regarding the many areas of exploration that still need to be examined with an open mind, curiosity and the belief that each person has something of significance to add to the discussion. And, by the way, don't forget to think outside the box. Should you choose to do this, you will have a process for continual renewal and learning that will continue for the rest of your life. Should you choose not to bother or to leave it to the experts, then the world will be less because of that fact. The choice is yours.

Websites on Community Economic Development

www.coop.org.ica—This is the Web site of the International Cooperative Alliance, an international nongovernmental organization that unites, represents and serves cooperatives throughout the world. Located in Geneva, Switzerland, the organization has over 230 member organizations in 100 countries representing 730 million cooperators.

www.socialinvertment.ca—This group's home page provides information on required investment amounts, length of investment, rates of return, fund management and social mandates.

www.ced.ns.ca—This site contains information on co-operatives, community economic development, business development corporations and community self-finance, with links to like-minded business development organizations and contacts throughout the world.

www.policyalternatives.ca—This site addresses such issues as: a) securing the future of public health care; b) an action plan for Kyoto; c) wealth inequality in Canada; and d) the gaps and blind spots in news coverage.

www.cgdev.org/—Center for Global Development—Provides information about our ongoing research projects, data sets and working papers.

www.eurodat.org/—European Network on Debt and Development—Umbrella for developing non-government organizations working for national economic and international financing policies that achieve poverty eradication. Provides research, lists of conferences and links to associated organizations.

www.odi.org.uk/pppg/—Poverty and Public Policy and Overseas Development Group—Provides research on poverty concepts and policies for managing poverty reduction at the country level.

www.odi.org.uk/iedg/—International Economic Development Institute—Provides research in development and foreign trade.

www.oecd.org/development/—Organization for Economic Cooperation and Development (OECD)—Presents OECD's publications and working papers about development like statistics, prospective studies or country surveys.

www.canadians.org—The Council of Canadians Web site—Provides a one-stop education and action site with the latest news releases, fact sheets and reports explaining key social, educational, economic and health issues.

Endnotes

Chapter 2

Michael Quinn Patton. *Qualitative Evaluation Methods*. Beverly Hills, CA.: Sage Publications, 1980.

———. *Practical Evaluation.* Beverly Hills, CA: Sage Publications, 1982.

———. *Utilization Focused Evaluation.* Beverly Hills, CA: Sage Publications, 1986.

Chapter 6

1. Simon Kuzosts, , *The New Republic*. October 20, 1962, cited in Cobb, Clifford, Ted Haistead and Jonathan Rowe. “If the GDP Is Up, Why Is America Down?” *Atlantic Monthly*. October, 1995, page 67.

2. Robert Kennedy, *Recapturing America's Moral Vision.* March 18, 1968, in *RFK: Collected Speeches*, Viking Press, 1993.

3. Signatories include Robert Dorfman, professor emeritus, Harvard University; Robert Heilbroner, professor emeritus, New School for Social Research; Herbert Simon, Nobel Laureate, 1978; Partha Dasgupta, Oxford University; Robert Eisner, former president, American Economics Association; Mohan Munasinghe, chief, Environmental Policy and Research Division, World Bank; Stephen Marglin and Juliet Schor, Harvard University; Don Paarlberg, professor emeritus, Purdue University; Emile Van Lennep, former secretary general, OECD; Maurice Strong, chair, Ontario Hydro, and secretary general, Rio Earth Summit; and Daniel Goeudevert, former chairman and president, Volkswagen AG. Full text and signatory list available from Redefining Progress, 1904 Franklin St., Oakland, CA 94612.

4. This data is from a detailed 223-page "Cost of Crime" report that is available through the GPI Atlantic Web site at www.gpiatlantic.org. Readers will find fully referenced sources for facts and statistics cited here in that report. The present purpose is simply to use some of those statistics for illustrative purposes to demonstrate how the GPI treats crime costs very differently from our standard economic growth measures.

Index

Acknowledgments

My wife Julie deserves a medal for standing by me through all the tough times, spread over thirty-six years, as do our four children (Dawn Michelle, Ann Marie, Danny, and Jimmy) for understanding why their father was so often away *at a meeting*.

Thanks to my niece, Kathy MacIntyre, (nicknamed by my editor as my "nice niece"), who made sure pictures were in an acceptable format and the table of contents and index are user friendly. She also did a great job of designing my web site and making it user friendly in preparation for my book release.

Thanks to my colleagues, Jaye and Don Castleden who worked so hard on early drafts of chapter two—out of which this book grew—and to Ronald Coleman, director of Genuine Progress Index, GPI Atlantic, for sharing the results of his research with me.

Thanks to my friends Donald Dunbar, Marianne Jewell, Mary M. Gillis and to members of NewERA and Don MacKay, the former mayor of Marathon, for reading early drafts of this book and giving me such valuable feedback.

Thank you to Francis Maloney, a lawyer from the neighboring community of Port Hood, a recent acquaintance I met during our community consultations on preparing a development plan for Inverness County, who meticulously went through every reference to ensure I had not violated any libel laws.

A very special thanks to my editor, Therese Hunolt, who was so helpful in a gentle caring way to ensure what I wrote is what I meant to say and then helped me say it succinctly. To Karen Maryanski who exceeded my expectations in designing the book cover, to my senior copyeditor, Margie Schlatter, who with a fresh perspective found a way to improve how things were communicated and the people at American Book Publishing Group for the guidelines, support, encouragement and help, you were so generous in polishing this material.

About the Author

With the exception of the time spent (after dropping out of high school) as a delivery salesman (grocery, milk and ice cream truck driver) and his year as a laborer at the Sydney Steel Plant (after five years in university), Angus spent his entire working life of thirty-six years being employed at the community level in community development organizational development (especially with nonprofit organizations); community-based economic development; education; and designing and conducting leadership training for civil servants, academics, business people and community leaders. Angus was active in the anti-war and civil-rights movements in the early sixties in the U.S., including the organization of Home Educational Visits—a movement begun in Chicago to change attitudes of the majority toward the minorities. He once spent forty-eight days on a vigil in front of the Lincoln Memorial in Washington, D.C., until the civil-rights legislation passed. Angus has worked on the war on poverty in Texas; as a public participation officer for a special NATO project in Canada; with First Nations across Canada including the Northwest Territories, northern Manitoba and northern Ontario, New Brunswick, Nova Scotia, Prince Edward Island, and Labrador. He changed jobs every three or four years and sometimes even more often. The theories presented in this book are heavily influenced by his experience in changing jobs frequently and working at the community level.

Angus earned his BA degree from Notre Dame University in South Bend, Indiana; did postgraduate work at Holy Cross College in Washington, D.C., the University of Michigan, the University of Texas and California State University; and obtained his master's degree in adult education from St. Francis Xavier University in Nova Scotia. He is also a graduate of the Coady International Institute in Antigonish, Nova Scotia.

For ten years, Angus was a professional member of the National Training Laboratories (NTL) Institute for Applied Behavioral Science in Virginia, where he taught corporate America on several of NTL's programs including Human

Interaction, Team Building, Complex Systems Change and Management Work Conferences for senior managers. He holds a professional designation as an economic developer (Ec.D.) from the University of Waterloo and the Economic Development Association of Canada (EDAC) and he is a Certified Human Resource Professional (CHRP) as well as a certified Program Leader for Kepner Tregoe's Planning, Problem Solving and Decision Making.

Angus and his wife of thirty-seven years, Julie, now live on Lake Ainslie in rural Cape Breton Island, where he works for the KLOG (Kanata Learning Opportunities Growth) Center. You may not recognize him if you were to meet him on the road going to or from a community meeting but you might recognize his car—it's the one with the front license plate that reads "I love L.A." No, L.A. does not stand for Los Angeles.